THE
GREATEST GAME
I EVER PLAYED

Art Direction: François Daxhelet
Cover Design: Leanne Gilbert
Graphic Design: Chantal Landry
Photo Research: Shea Berencsi
Project Editor: Ronnie Shuker
Fact-checkers: Malcolm Campbell & Casey Ippolito
Copy Editor: Rachel Villari
Proofreader: Luke Sawczak

Cover information:
  Ovechkin: John Russell/NHLI via Getty Images
  Crosby: Justin K. Aller/Getty Images
  Gordie Howe: O-Pee-Chee/HHOF (Back Cover)

Catalogue data available from Bibliothèque et Archives
nationales du Québec

EXCLUSIVE DISTRIBUTOR :

For Canada and the United States:
Simon & Schuster Canada
166 King Street East, Suite 300
Toronto, ON M5A 1J3
phone: (647) 427-8882
        1-800-387-0446
Fax: (647) 430-9446
simonandschuster.ca

09-16

© 2016, Juniper Publishing,
division of the Sogides Group Inc.,
a subsidiary of Québecor Média Inc.
(Montreal, Quebec)

Printed in Canada
All rights reserved

Legal deposit: 2065
National Library of Québec
National Library of Canada

ISBN 978-1-988002-30-9

 Conseil des Arts   Canada Council
du Canada   for the Arts

We gratefully acknowledge the support of the Canada
Council for the Arts for its publishing program.

We acknowledge the financial support of the
Government of Canada through the Canada Book Fund
for our publishing activities.

The Hockey News

THE
GREATEST GAME
I EVER PLAYED

40 EPIC TALES OF HOCKEY BRILLIANCE

— EDITED BY RONNIE SHUKER —

For K, the greatest...

TABLE OF CONTENTS

•••

FOREWORD

• • •

"I don't believe my greatest game is still ahead of me, still to be played. I know it is."
—Jaromir Jagr

You've got to have perspective when someone asks about the greatest game you ever played. When I was 20, I may have done something I thought was my best, but when I was 25 I didn't think that way anymore. Every game is the biggest, when you think about it. I might not remember what happened last night, but I'm looking forward to tomorrow, and I don't have a favorite game because every game is special to me. I prepare the same way every game. I have to play the same way every game. I try and play my best every time I go out there on the ice.

The fans look at things differently than players do. In a hockey game, I'm an actor, a performer. In movies or onstage, actors do the best they can in every performance. Actors don't control the story, but they do the best they can to perform their roles and be the best they can at all times. Yet even when actors give the best performances of their lives, if people don't like the movie or the script is bad, then, well, it doesn't work. Singers can be great, but fans of a new generation may not like them. A band that was huge in the 1970s can come in and put on a concert, and it could be the greatest music ever made – a terrific concert. Yet you'll have 18-year-olds in the audience going, "What was that garbage?"

To me, everything is subjective. I look at every game as a blessing. I might play the greatest game ever, but some people will find fault with it. Why? Because they want to. Or I can play the worst game ever and some people will see something good in it. Everything is subjective.

We're playing a game. Hockey is a game, and we're all making a good living playing it. How lucky are we? How many people get to play a game for a living? I know some players look at this as simply a job, and that's their right, but they're not going to last very long. You can't pretend that's all it is. Every person is different, and some will look at this as simply a paycheque, but there are just things you can't control.

Some guys were shoved into playing a sport when they were young, and though they didn't particularly like it, they didn't have much choice. A lot of people are pushed into hockey who may not like playing it and don't want to be there. Look at cultures that have arranged marriage, where your parents decide who you marry. You may learn to love the wife you had forced upon you, but it could take 50 years.

In my case, I was pushed into hockey, but I liked it. I was lucky. My arranged marriage was to a beautiful woman, if you will. I started playing when I was five, and I loved it from the start, but I knew if I wasn't playing hockey, there were other things I would be doing on our farm, and those things were no fun. Hockey, though, was always fun. I didn't want to be on the farm all day. I would rather be on the ice. I just loved being out there.

Recently I was asked, "What motivates you on a day-to-day basis?" I didn't exactly know how to answer that question. For almost 40 years, I've been playing hockey. I was five when I started, and no one knows when I will stop.

When the guy asked me the question, I thought about it for a second. I don't think you need motivation to play hockey. You don't need motivation to live. You just live. You do things that make you happy. There's no need for motivation there.

There are millions of people who would be happy to do what I do just for one day. There are millions of people who go to a "regular" job, and after working all day they go and play hockey with their friends. And they have to pay to do that. Do they need motivation? No. They love it so they do it. If you need to be motivated to do something, you're probably not happy doing it, so that kind of question surprises me.

Nobody cares what you did yesterday. All anyone cares about is what you're doing for them today or tomorrow. Yesterday? That's in the past, and whatever happened, happened. I can't change it, you can't change it, and everyone knows what happened because it's in books or on the internet. You can read all about it. So yesterday doesn't matter. In talking about the past, "if" doesn't matter. There is no "if." It is what it is.

Someone will ask, "Would you like to have done something differently?" I say no, because you couldn't do something differently, or you would have done that thing. Everyone is smarter once something is done, but you make your decisions in a split second. If you changed up something in the moment, the end result might have been different. You live with the decisions you make in the moment.

I know I'm not the same player I was 20 years ago. So what? If you want to keep playing at a high level as you age, then slow things down. You can slow things down a lot, but it's up to you whether you want to do it.

The worst thing I could say about getting old in this game is there is no room for error. My father told me there would be a lot of jealous people out there, people waiting for you to fail, even people who will be happy if you fail. "Don't make them happy" – that's what he always said. I don't want to give those people the satisfaction of seeing me make a mistake. Yet it may happen, I don't know. I can't control how my life goes, where God puts me.

My father also told me that, if I am like him, I would be at my strongest from age 38 to 50. He told me that when I was 18. I later told that to former Rangers GM Glen Sather when I was 36 and still playing in New York. He didn't listen. He only wanted to give me one year. But I knew I had many more in me.

So, again, what is my motivation?

I love this game. I love playing it. It makes life exciting for me – everything about it. For me to play, I need to be having fun, and to have fun, to continue being the kind of player I need to be, I know that as things slow down I have to work harder. The only rule I have is to work hard off the ice and prepare for the game.

The game is much easier to play when you're prepared. I hate to be unprepared for anything. Working hard doesn't bother me. I like to beat up my body – I enjoy it. You can control the body when you beat it up. It doesn't control you. You just have to make sure you produce and give everything every game. Some days will be better than others, but you can only control yourself and what you put into the game.

BY JAROMIR JAGR

INTRODUCTION

•••

You've got to love Jaromir Jagr. When our Florida Panthers correspondent, George Richards, asked him which game he considers his greatest ever, Jagr initially sidestepped the question, saying his best was still yet to come, even though he is in his mid-40s and has already played more than 2,000 games throughout his surefire Hall of Fame career.

So we called Jagr on what we thought was a bluff and asked him to envision his greatest game ever and describe it to us. It turns out the man wasn't bluffing at all. He agreed to our request, and what followed were his stream-of-consciousness views on hockey and life that you just read in the foreword. It's vintage Jagr waxing poetic on the game and weaving philosophical about life.

Although Jagr doesn't want to revel in the past, since it won't help him in the present, hockey fans sure do. Nostalgia is part of our DNA as lovers of the world's greatest game. We're constantly looking ahead: to opening day, the Winter Classic, the All-Star Game, the trade deadline, the end of the season, the start of the playoffs, the crowning of another Stanley Cup champion, the draft, the first day of free agency – and then we do it all again the following season.

But during the downtimes, we like to remember the moments that have made this game so great. And that's what we've done in *The Greatest Game I Ever Played*.

We've narrowed our focus to some of the best single-game performances in the history of hockey. Many of the most memorable are here: Jordan Eberle's late-game heroics against Russia in the world juniors, Dominik Hasek's superhuman goaltending in shutting down Canada at the Nagano Games, Darryl Sittler's record 10-point game against Don Cherry and the Bruins, Red Berenson's six-goal showcase on the road in Philadelphia, Bill Mosienko's 21 seconds of fame that catapulted him into hockey's Hall of Fame, Maurice Richard's five-goal game against the Maple Leafs in the playoffs and Joe Malone's record seven-goal game in the early days of the NHL. These are the stuff of legend, and their stories are retold here.

But we didn't want to stop there. Beyond the obvious epic performances and behind the stars that pulled them off were games and players, many now long forgotten, that featured feats of hockey glory over 60 minutes (and sometimes more). Before going on to a successful NHL career, André Savard had a record 12-point game in the QMJHL, while Kimbi Daniels, who turned out to be a career minor-leaguer, scored all seven of his team's goals one day in the WHL. Former NHL fighter Mick Vukota, feeling depressed about not contributing more to his team beyond chucking knuckles, went out and scored a natural hat trick in exactly five minutes after receiving a pep talk from the team's leading scorer. Eight years before playing in the longest game in KHL history, Michael Leighton faced 101 shots in the longest AHL game ever. And did you know that a few years before Sittler's 10-point game a fellow by the name of Jim Harrison hit double digits one night in the World Hockey Association? Few do because no radio or television footage of the game exists today.

Even when it came to some of hockey's biggest names and best players, many of them went way off the board (though not quite as far as Jagr did) when asked to choose their greatest game ever.

Take Martin Brodeur, for example. He could've chosen any number of games that led to his three Stanley Cups, two Olympic gold medals or one of the numerous records he set during his career. Instead, he chose, of all games, a loss in his rookie season, because he said it helped him learn what it takes to win. On behalf of their father, Gordie, the Howe brothers (Mark and Marty) selected an exhibition affair that Gordie got kicked out of midway through the game, because they had made hockey history as a family. Chris Pronger, meanwhile, chose a game in which he didn't even hit the scoresheet yet logged the most minutes in arguably the most pressure-packed game ever played in Canada.

What you won't see in the pages that follow are basic blow-by-blow game reports. *The Hockey News'* cadre of correspondents has gone beyond the scoresheets to find the stories behind the games. Mike Brophy recounts two of the Stastny brothers' (Peter and Anton) harrowing defection from Czechoslovakia the summer before their dual eight-point nights in the same game as rookies. Josh Elliott details the torturous bike ride that propelled Hayley Wickenheiser and Canada's national women's team to gold at the Sochi Games. Ken Campbell tells the heartwarming tale of Milt Schmidt being carried off the ice on his archrivals' shoulders after his last game before being shipped out to fight in the Second World War. And Jason Buckland describes former referee Kerry Fraser's best performance as a zebra – one that involves an itchy body rash and a Game 7 in the Battle of Quebec.

Those stories, and many more, are to come. But we start by tipping our hats to hockey's two biggest stars today – 'Sid' and 'Ovie' – and the night they went goal-for-goal in their greatest game ever against each other.

BY RONNIE SHUKER

ALEX OVECHKIN & SIDNEY CROSBY

MAY 4, 2009

WASHINGTON 4 vs. PITTSBURGH 3

• • •

Burdened by never-ending comparisons, the NHL's two biggest stars delivered epic performances as they went head-to-head – and traded hat trick for hat trick – in the heat of the playoffs.

"You don't see that happen too often – two hat tricks in a game. And then there was everything that was going on with that series and the buildup between him and I."
—Sidney Crosby

"There were all kinds of comparisons between Sid and I, and the fans hated each other."
—Alex Ovechkin

Sidney Crosby and Alex Ovechkin have repeatedly recoiled from comparisons to each other. Because of the lost lockout season, they entered the NHL together in 2005-06, and the comparisons have continued ever since. They were a pair of generational talents, consecutive first-overall draft picks in 2004 and 2005 that fortuitously fell to the Washington Capitals and Pittsburgh Penguins, who had both faded into irrelevance during the early part of the millennium.

The questions and comparisons began almost immediately and have never really stopped. Could these two young stars bring the NHL back from its work stoppage? That hype finally peaked in a 2009 Stanley Cup playoff series that was four years in the making.

Crosby and Ovechkin recorded memorable hat tricks in Game 2 of that Eastern Conference semifinal. Even though the constant individual comparisons still rankled them, the two phenoms were just entering their primes and pushing each

other to new heights. "It was fun. That's what makes sports exciting," Crosby said. "A game like that, it's fun when you look back."

Crosby and the Penguins had lost to the Detroit Red Wings in the Stanley Cup final the year before in six games and were looking to get back. Ovechkin and the Capitals, meanwhile, were coming off their first playoff series win since 1998, having beaten the New York Rangers in seven games the round before. Both teams knew that if they could make it past each other, a title was within their reach.

In the end, Pittsburgh was the team that won the Cup that season. The Penguins outlasted Washington in seven games, swept the underdog Carolina Hurricanes in the Eastern Conference final and then defeated the Red Wings in a Stanley Cup rematch.

But during that memorable second-round series with the Capitals, it was Game 2 that left jaws agape. Washington won that day, 4-3, at Verizon Center, as the NHL's two biggest stars went head-to-head in their best game ever against each other.

Crosby opened the scoring in the first period and recorded his hat trick with 31 seconds left to pull his team to within a goal. But Ovechkin's relentless play eventually pushed the Caps over the top. "It was a great opponent and a huge win for us," Ovechkin said. "I don't think about it a lot now, because it was a tough series for us to lose."

The two faces of the NHL produced brilliant performances on national television, and the league was thrilled to see its marquee names fighting with the stakes so high in the playoffs. Crosby had won the Hart Trophy as the NHL's most valuable player in 2007. Ovechkin took that trophy in 2008 and would again in 2009.

The two teams also had a history, which only added intrigue. The Penguins had devastated Washington time and again in the post-season with six series wins over 11 years between 1991 and 2001. Twice during that stretch the Capitals blew 3-1 series leads to Pittsburgh and another time were up 2-0 and lost.

Ovechkin didn't care about the past entering that Monday night game in Washington, though. He was just a kid in Russia when those losses happened, after all, so to him it was ancient history. But the pain lingers still from the 2009 defeat – so much so that he hasn't watched highlights from Game 2 since the day it happened.

That victory gave Washington a 2-0 series lead, but it lost the next three games. Ovechkin had three assists in a dramatic Game 6 overtime win in Pittsburgh, but the very next night the series ended in more misery for the Capitals after a 6-2 blowout loss at home in Game 7.

Still, it's Game 2 that fans remember. As one former Caps player said, everybody was already expecting a "gunfight" between two of the most skilled players in the world before the series even began. The way it actually happened was almost too good to be true. Ovechkin finished the series with eight goals

and six assists, while Crosby had eight goals and five assists.

There were other players on the ice, but in that second game Crosby and Ovechkin turned into heavyweight boxers, throwing one haymaker after another until the final horn sounded. And while neither player has ever enjoyed those inevitable comparisons with each other, both acknowledge that they pushed each other to a higher level in that game, not because each wanted to one-up the other, but because they knew that's what was necessary for a victory. It turned out to be true for Ovechkin that day but also for Crosby during the entire series and championship run.

For once, the rivalry that was always hyped between the two men finally meant something more on the ice than just a regular season game between opponents in different divisions that would soon be forgotten. It went far beyond a stats race for most goals or points, and both men were keenly aware of it. "More so when you're going head-to-head, just because it's fresh and you see him every shift," Crosby said. "I understand that my job is to score, but I also have to make sure that I'm good defensively because this is a guy that can make us pay."

Crosby scored the first goal of the game, sniping a point shot on the power play. Ovechkin answered early in the second period with a one-timer, only to see Crosby again put his team on top, making it 2-1 a few minutes later by slamming home a rebound in front of the net.

After David Steckel tied the game for Washington, Ovechkin took control with just over seven minutes left in the third period. He put Washington ahead for good with a power play goal after a faceoff win and a quick pass from teammate Mike Green. Even with the crowd roaring at jet engine decibel levels, Ovechkin distinctly remembers hearing the screams of an incensed Penguins player who believed he'd been tripped by Caps left winger Alexander Semin on the faceoff. That subtle play definitely kept Matt Cooke

> "I 100-PERCENT KNEW I HAD TO PLAY WELL THAT NIGHT AND HELP MY TEAM. IT'S A SERIES I DON'T LIKE TO REMEMBER, BUT THAT DAY IT WAS GOOD."

from reaching Ovechkin, though it probably wouldn't have mattered. Green's pass was right in Ovechkin's wheelhouse and the puck was away in the blink of an eye and immediately past a helpless Marc-André Fleury in goal.

Just over two minutes later, Ovechkin added another one at even strength, employing his classic inside-out move and using Penguins defenseman and fellow Russian Sergei Gonchar as a screen to whip a shot past Fleury from 20 feet out, temporarily upstaging Crosby. "When it's like that in the playoffs, it's a good matchup," Ovechkin said. "You have to play better than he does or you lose."

After Ovechkin scored that third goal to put Washington ahead 4-2, the Verizon Center crowd became so excited it just kept throwing hats out of the stands. The long delay to clear the ice infuriated Crosby, who pleaded with the officials to have the P.A. announcer tell the crowd to stop throwing hats. The normally reserved superstar had let Ovechkin's performance get under his skin. The rivalry, for the first time, had become a very personal affair.

Crosby struck back with his hat trick goal at 19:29, batting a puck out of midair to make it 4-3. But it was too late. The Capitals killed off the final 31 seconds, and the crowd was left roaring its approval with its team in control of the series.

Ovechkin finished with an incredible 12 shots on goal – more than Crosby (five) and teammate Evgeni Malkin (six) combined. Two of Crosby's goals came on the power play. "I 100-percent knew I had to play well that night and help my team," Ovechkin said. "It's a series I don't like to remember, but that day it was good."

Other young phenoms in other cities have since risen to stardom and won Stanley Cups, but that was exactly what the NHL hoped for. The league needed Crosby and Ovechkin to be the vanguard for a generation of talented, young players who could intrigue fans and build the sport. They've had better individual performances throughout their careers, but on that captivating spring night in Washington, the top two players in the sport brought out the elite in each other. "If you're competitive and you understand the situation, it should bring the best out in you," Crosby said. "It's not something that grabs your entire focus, but you're aware of it. I think that's a good thing."

BY BRIAN MCNALLY

JORDAN EBERLE

JANUARY 3, 2009

CANADA 6 VS. RUSSIA 5

• • •

There are generational moments that give you goosebumps every time you think of them – like the one Eberle gave his country with 5.4 seconds remaining.

"People still ask me about that goal all the time, all these years later. I've had other really good games, but because of the stage and the situation – Canada-Russia, five seconds left and it looks like we're going to lose – people remember that game and that goal the most. It's a different feeling when the whole country is cheering for you. That was definitely a special night."
—Jordan Eberle

O nly two words are needed to set the stage: Canada-Russia.

Dating back to 1972, when it was Canada-Soviet Union, that is all the billing that has ever been necessary. When hockey fans around the world see Canada-Russia, they know they are about to witness something special.

And at the 2009 World Junior Championship semifinal in Ottawa between the longtime rivals, it was a Paul Henderson special. An 18-year-old Jordan Eberle began that night as a little known Regina Pats forward and ended it as one of the greatest heroes in Canadian hockey history. "More than anything in that game I just remember the energy in the building," he said. "And I remember feeling really good."

Eberle has delivered on other big stages, like when he scored twice in just over a minute late in the third to turn a 5-3 deficit into a 5-5 tie against the United States in the 2010 gold medal game. And his first NHL goal is still dropping jaws on YouTube.

But the 2009 semifinal was Canada-Russia, and the Canadians were hanging by a thread. Their shot at a fifth consecutive gold medal was about to die on home ice at the hands of their most bitter rival. "There were such incredible momentum shifts," Eberle said. "We would score and they would score, we would score and they would score, we would score and they would score. It was an incredible game."

The mood swings were as fast as they were violent. Canada scored first at 2:02, Russia replied at 5:18. Canada scored again at 7:04, Russia at 7:20. Canada late in the second, Russia early in the third. Canada with 14:16 left in the game, Russia with 13:38.

Then, in a game in which the Canadians had never trailed, the unthinkable happened. Russia scored late, at 17:40 of the third, to take a 5-4 lead. The hosts were in serious trouble – 2:20 away from the kind of a heartbreak that would torture them forever. Then 2:20 trickled down to one minute.

It was over. Or at least it should have been.

Like Henderson's goal 37 years before, the circumstances were lined up perfectly for the Canadians, as if the hockey gods wanted to see what they would do with one last shot. Russia fired at the empty net from the wrong side of center. They missed, and it was called for icing.

The Russians had two attempts to clear the puck and win the game with less than 15 seconds left, but they couldn't. "Ryan Ellis made a hell of a play to keep it in along the blueline, then John Tavares just backhanded it into the slot and (Russian defenseman) Dmitry Kulikov tried to grab it and missed," Eberle said. "There are so many things that had to go right for that to happen. I just happened to be in the right spot at the right time."

Eberle grabbed the puck on his forehand, brought it to his backhand and lifted the tying goal past diving netminder Vadim Zhelobnyuk with 5.4 seconds left to play. All TSN's Gord Miller could say, amid the deafening roar in Ottawa, was, "Can you believe it?"

> ## "THERE ARE SO MANY THINGS THAT HAD TO GO RIGHT FOR THAT TO HAPPEN. I JUST HAPPENED TO BE IN THE RIGHT SPOT AT THE RIGHT TIME."

Because nobody could. Not even Eberle. "I remember just getting tackled by P.K. (Subban)," Eberle said. "I couldn't believe it. People ask what it was like to score, and to be honest I don't really remember. You put the puck in the net, and it's just, 'Holy crap! What just happened?' The crowd was so loud."

Years later, he can still hear it. "I have the picture in the house of that goal, and my favorite part of it is just seeing the fans' faces in the background. They're going absolutely crazy."

Then, as if to tie a bow on his performance, Eberle, who had also scored in the second period, scored the game-winning goal in the shootout.

Two days later in the gold medal game, he had a goal and two assists against Sweden, giving Canada its fifth straight championship.

BY ROB TYCHKOWSKI

GORDIE, MARK & MARTY HOWE

SEPTEMBER 27, 1973

LOS ANGELES 3 VS. HOUSTON 2

•••

Bored out of his mind after retiring, Mr. Hockey returned to play with
his two teenaged sons, forging the game's first hockey family.
And right from the get-go, the sons' legendary dad showed them how to survive
in the early years of the wild World Hockey Association.

"Say, Bill, how would you like to have three Howes?"
—Gordie Howe

North Carolina's Greensboro Coliseum had hosted a lot of hockey by 1973, mostly from the rough and tumble Eastern League, the minor-pro circuit that would soon inspire the film *Slap Shot*. The fans who came there on Sept. 27 for a pre-season game between the World Hockey Association's Houston Aeros and Los Angeles Sharks saw some of that and something more – a fabled, then 45-year-old Hall of Famer, still blessed with sufficient talent and toughness, coming out of retirement to become the first pro athlete to play alongside his sons as teammates.

Ask Marty and Mark Howe to select one game as their favorite from the seven seasons (six in the WHA and one in the NHL) that they played alongside their father, Gordie, and you're presenting them with a nearly impossible task. But in that first professional outing in what Mark calls "the wild, goon-laden WHA," they realized a family dream.

If that game made history, so did the process of getting the younger Howes into the rebellious WHA, fresh off its first season. Scouts from everywhere had watched them win the Memorial Cup

at the Montreal Forum with the Toronto Marlboros in early May, where the 18-year-old Mark was named the tournament MVP. But teenagers like him and his 19-year-old brother were "off-limits" to the NHL, which had agreed with the Canadian Amateur Hockey Association not to recruit players before they turned 20.

Their mother Colleen – who acknowledged that her "temper and directness" often amused her more laconic husband – had openly railed against that rule, believing that any teenager good enough to play pro hockey should have the chance. And at the Montreal Forum, she had directed her plea toward Gordie's former Red Wings teammate Bill Dineen, now scouting in his capacity as Houston's coach. She asked, "Bill, did your league ever reach an agreement to abide by the age minimum?" Dineen paused, then replied he didn't think it had.

The Aeros' lawyers examined the issue and believed teens were fair game. Not surprisingly, shock pervaded the WHA draft proceedings later that month when Houston selected Mark as their first-round pick. Colleen phoned Mark – slow to start after celebrating the Memorial Cup win – in

Toronto, and his first blurry thought was, " 'Who? What league?' My entire 18 years on Earth to that point were focused on one thing, and that was playing pro hockey in the NHL."

He also told her he wasn't going anywhere without Marty. Colleen later wrote, "His concern for his older brother made my eyes blur." They needn't have worried, though. Houston would stun observers a second time, selecting Marty in the 12th round.

But the biggest bomb was still to drop: Gordie joining his sons two years after completing an unparalleled 25-season career. He'd retired in 1971 as hockey's all-time leading scorer, taking an unfulfilling public relations job for the Red Wings – referring to his position as "Vice-President in Charge of Paperclips" – and growing increasingly unhappy. When he raised the prospect of returning, his spouse was initially skeptical. He responded with characteristic understatement: "I don't know, Colleen. It would be fun." Then, during a fateful phone call with Dineen to discuss his sons' futures, Gordie offhandedly offered to lace 'em up again, giving Dineen and the Aeros three Howes in Houston.

There was nothing offhand about Dineen's reply. "Hell, yes!" he said.

So the grey-haired father and his long-haired sons signed with Houston in June 1973, dumbfounding the hockey world. Their new city greeted them with a banner hung from a downtown skyscraper that read "Welcome to Howestown," as the three prepared for a unique challenge. "After a few tough weeks of camp, Dad started to look like his old self," Mark said. "Marty caught on and fit into the league faster than I did."

In September, the Aeros initially travelled to New York's Madison Square Garden for a WHA showcase of 20-minute mini-games featuring Winnipeg, New England and the New York Golden Blades, who wore white skates. "That didn't seem right to me," Marty recalled.

Then it was down to Greensboro for the trio's first real 60-minute contest. Although the teenagers would be facing grown men, there was no particular pre-game guidance from father to sons. "Gordie seldom, if ever, offered unsolicited advice," Mark said.

"I don't remember much advice from Dad other than 'Keep your head up,' " Marty said. "I didn't think much about older competition as we had always played against competition that was two years older than we were most of our lives. I was six-feet and 190 pounds, so I was strong and big enough to hold my own."

Good thing he was, as this would be no fairy-tale beginning. "In exhibition games back then, there were always extra guys looking to make a team with their fists, not their skills," Marty said. "And what better way to make a name for yourself than to fight Gordie Howe?"

Dineen put the three Howes out for the opening faceoff – Gordie on right wing, Mark on left wing and Marty on defense – and as the puck dropped, so did the gloves of an eager Sharks unknown across from the Gordie, anxious to try the old man. "C'mon, Howe," he taunted.

Gordie had long practiced what he called "religious hockey," maintaining it was better to give than receive. "As soon as the words came out, Gordie's stick landed on his forehead, right between the eyes," Marty said. "He wasn't wearing a helmet, and he fell to his knees. Blood squirted from under his hands as he held his head. The thought that went through my mind was, 'So this is pro hockey.' "

Handed a major high-sticking penalty, Gordie served his time. And when he left the penalty box, Dineen kept him out for the next faceoff. Another Shark lined up across from Gordie, and as the puck dropped, he too began to drop his stick and utter, "C'mon, H—." Before he could finish, Gordie's stick smacked him in the forehead directly between the eyes. He fell holding his head as blood squirted once more onto the ice. "This time, Gordie didn't go directly to the penalty box," Marty said. "He stood there for a second, looking at the guy. He shook his head, then took a long look at their bench before heading to the penalty box."

The game settled down somewhat afterward, and Gordie skated without incident. In the second period, however, trouble brewed again.

Gordie was backchecking, and he wasn't completely back in shape, being 45 and not having played for two years.

As Marty recounts, Gordie pulled one of his old tricks in which he would "tickle the chin" of whoever he was trying to catch with his stick. Reaching out with one hand, positioning his stick under the player's armpit, he'd lift up the blade, forcing the player to raise his head toward the rafters. "It's impossible to maintain your speed if you keep lifting your head up," Marty said. "He was like a surgeon the way he could control that piece of lumber."

This time, however, Dr. Howe's stick made a small incision on the puck carrier's chin, drawing blood. A third high-sticking major – another sort of Gordie Howe hat trick – meant automatic ejection.

On the very next shift, with Mr. Hockey now out of the game and the Sharks emboldened, a bench-clearing brawl broke out, one casualty being Marty's defense partner Dunc McCallum, whose leg was fractured when he squared off against L.A.'s Steve Sutherland. McCallum missed the entire season. "It was the first time I understood how much Gordie could control a game with his presence on the ice," Marty said.

If these WHA upstarts planned on building reputations by taking on Mr. Hockey, Gordie wasn't going to comply. In each of the next five pre-season games, he lined up for the opening faceoff and, unprovoked, clocked the guy across

"IN EXHIBITION GAMES BACK THEN, THERE WERE ALWAYS EXTRA GUYS LOOKING TO MAKE A TEAM WITH THEIR FISTS, NOT THEIR SKILLS. AND WHAT BETTER WAY TO MAKE A NAME FOR YOURSELF THAN TO FIGHT GORDIE HOWE?"

from him. Word quickly got around the league. "He was making a statement and it worked," Marty remembered. "By the sixth game, the guy lined up six feet away from him. Gordie now had all the room he wanted."

Despite the rocky start, things worked out quite well. Gordie played 70 games that season, totalled 100 points, and deservedly won the league's MVP award, which two years later would be renamed the Gordie Howe Trophy. Selected as top WHA rookie, Mark didn't take long to find his place as a pro, eventually moving back to defense as an NHLer and forging a Hall of Fame career of his own. Marty would be a plus-135 in six WHA seasons and the three Howes would lead the Aeros to consecutive Avco Cup championships in their first two WHA campaigns.

With Colleen overseeing much of her family's business, the Howes played another three seasons in Houston, then three together for the New England/ Hartford Whalers, the last of which marked Gordie's return to the NHL after the WHA's demise. He was 52 and a grandfather when he finally retired for good in 1980.

A banner now hangs in the rafters of the XL Center in Hartford honoring Gordie, Colleen, Marty and Mark as "Hockey's First Family." That rowdy night in Greensboro made the "First Family" a reality.

BY STU HACKEL

MARTIN BRODEUR

APRIL 27, 1994

BUFFALO 1 vs. NEW JERSEY 0

•••

With a record 1,266 games played between the pipes, it should come as no surprise that Brodeur considers his best ever to be a marathon quadruple-overtime playoff affair, regardless of the score.

"I could talk to you about the Olympics against the U.S. in 2002.
I could talk to you about my first Stanley Cup in 1995. But when people ask me about the
best game I played, for me, at that stage of my career, I wouldn't give it up. I think it's
interesting because people don't expect you to pick a loss, but it was a good game for me
because I learned a lot about how to survive."
—Martin Brodeur

To win Game 6 of the 1994 Eastern Conference quarterfinal, Martin Brodeur knew that he would have to shut out the Sabres. That's because in net for Buffalo was Dominik Hasek.

The 29-year-old Hasek was coming off a 30-win regular season, leading to his first Vezina Trophy as the NHL's top goalie and a second-place finish for the Hart Trophy as league MVP. Brodeur, meanwhile, was in his first season as the New Jersey Devils' No. 1 goaltender and would take home the Calder Trophy as the top rookie that season. But he was still only two weeks shy of turning 22 when he suited up for his first NHL playoff series, and now here he was going toe-to-toe – or trading toe-save for toe-save, rather – with the best goalie in the game at the time.

New Jersey held a 3-2 lead in the series as it shifted back to Buffalo's Memorial Auditorium on April 27, 1994. The Devils wanted to clinch the series that night so they could go home, not just back to New Jersey but to their own houses. The club had a policy under longtime GM Lou Lamoriello of staying in hotels during the post-season, even when they were hosting games in the Meadowlands. Cell phones were still a couple years away, so messages for the players had to be left with the hotel, and they were screened by coach Jacques Lemaire. "We were really in jail with the Devils," Brodeur said. "We were 12 days into the playoffs, and we hadn't gone home yet. The only time we saw our family was for five minutes after the game, and then we had to jump on the bus. So for us it was an opportunity – if we win this, we go home. Everybody was like, 'Guys, let's bear down.' "

Beginning in the warmup, Brodeur's night was playing out in slow motion because he had yet to face this level of pressure. And it would only intensify as the game wore on and the players wore out. The Devils were trained to execute their defensive trap and accustomed to low-scoring games. "But 0-0 was over the top," Brodeur admitted.

The goalie's gear was being dried between periods while his thoughts tumbled in his head. The visiting dressing room at The Aud was divided, so Brodeur was separated from some of his teammates. As the game went into overtime, however, one teammate who was a healthy scratch that night paid him a visit.

Veteran Bernie Nicholls walked in and told Brodeur, "Kid, you shut them down this period, and we're going to win the game for sure." No problem, replied Brodeur, who upheld his end of the bargain for another 20 minutes.

Still, the game was scoreless heading into the second overtime. In came Nicholls again, telling Brodeur, "I was just joking before, but I'm telling you now if you shut them out this period, we're going to win, for sure." Brodeur remained spotless, but still the game was scoreless going into a third overtime. "Go for three!" Nicholls exclaimed.

Indeed, Brodeur kept New Jersey alive through three OTs – the equivalent of two full games. Exhausted, he was anticipating another pep talk, but this time when Nicholls walked in he only said, "Kid, you're on your own."

As Brodeur took the crease for the fourth overtime, he was thinking about the epic Game 7 battle between the Washington Capitals and New York Islanders in 1987, which Pat LaFontaine mercifully ended in the fourth overtime with a goal to give the Isles a 3-2 victory. "I had that in my mind... like, 'That's how these fans are feeling,'" Brodeur said. "We're in the wee hours and people were sleeping in the rink. We're going back and forth, Dominik and I, making save after save. It was surreal."

Then it happened.

Five minutes and 43 seconds into the fourth OT, Buffalo's Jason Dawe put a puck in front of the crease from behind the net, and with Brodeur on his bottom, the Sabres' Dave Hannan flipped in a backhander to win the game 1-0. Brodeur had made 49 saves up to that point, but had little chance at stopping No. 50. His counterpart, Hasek, finished with 70 saves in what went down as one of the best goaltending duals in playoff history. "It went on and on and on, and finally we failed," Brodeur said. "But to drag it on for so long, I was pretty proud of myself. I was like, 'There's no way we're going to lose this series.' We won Game 7, by the way, just to bring that up."

New Jersey edged Buffalo 2-1 in the decisive series finale. The Devils won another round, but fell in the Eastern Conference final to the eventual Stanley Cup champion New York Rangers. Still, Brodeur said that to this day, every time he returns to Buffalo, he has great memories of a loss that catapulted his career.

BY JEREMY RUTHERFORD

> ## "WE'RE IN THE WEE HOURS AND PEOPLE WERE SLEEPING IN THE RINK. WE'RE GOING BACK AND FORTH, DOMINIK AND I, MAKING SAVE AFTER SAVE. IT WAS SURREAL."

CHRIS PRONGER

---- FEBRUARY 28, 2010 ----

CANADA 3 VS. UNITED STATES 2

•••

Pronger's 18-year career is littered with accolades and hardware, but his most memorable game was one in which he didn't even hit the scoresheet. After his sour start to the 2010 Olympics, victory tasted that much sweeter when he helped Canada take home gold at home.

"It took me a while to figure out how to answer the question of what my greatest game was, because it's not an easy question. But the 2010 Olympic gold medal game against Team USA in Vancouver would be my pick. Early on in the tournament, my mind was elsewhere at times, but as it went along, I was able to refocus and get my game back when it mattered the most. And that game stands out – the magnitude of it, being in Canada, the pressure on the team, the buildup to that Olympics and the debacle that was the Canadian team in 2006. We as a country needed to get ourselves back on the right track. And at the end of the day, you're in a gold medal game, and experience matters in a game of that magnitude. I think my experience brought my game to the forefront. And the right team won."
—Chris Pronger

I t is indicative of Chris Pronger's dedication to his mission as a defenseman that he believes the greatest game he ever played ended with the following statistics to his name: zero goals, zero assists, zero plus-minus rating.

As great as Pronger was, he was never a player who could threaten Darryl Sittler's NHL-record 10-point game. But Pronger's pick for his greatest game did end with him collecting a different honor: He led his Canadian countrymen in ice time and won his second Olympic gold medal.

To truly understand why the Hall of Fame blueliner picked the gold medal final at the 2010 Games, you need to grasp how players judge themselves: not necessarily simply by the results

of any single 60-minute stretch of play – or, in this case, the 67:40 it took before Sidney Crosby scored the game- and championship-winner on American star netminder Ryan Miller – but as part of a larger process.

In this instance, it wasn't just any process, either. Rather, it was a hyper-intense, pressure-packed process watched by the world and staged before a rabid Vancouver throng whose lust for gold channelled the nation's obsession with atoning for Canada's calamitous seventh-place finish four years prior in Turin. And in Pronger's case, what made the process special enough to call it his best were the struggles he needed to overcome in order to be on the ice more than any other Canadian player when the stakes were highest.

For one thing, he entered the tournament tired and worn down. He was 35 years old at that point and heavily played by the Philadelphia Flyers, who'd acquired him from Anaheim in the summer of 2009 and were playing him anywhere from 25 to 30 minutes a game. But players who've done what Pronger had already done – he'd won a Stanley Cup, a Hart Trophy and a Norris Trophy and ended Canada's half-century Olympic gold drought in 2002 – know better than anyone how to push through fatigue. Familiar woes may stress you out as an elite player, but at least you have a template for moving beyond it.

No, far more troubling to Pronger was the system deployed by Canadian coach Mike Babcock in his first Olympic Games behind the bench. In the three Olympics he'd played before 2010, Pronger had worked under Marc Crawford and Pat Quinn – well-respected and veteran hockey men who adhered to a more traditional approach to the game, one with which Pronger was well-acquainted. But Babcock brought something different to the table, and Pronger was unsure of what he was looking at. "A lot of the systems we were playing I'd never played before," Pronger said. "I was a little behind the 8-ball in what we were trying to do, killing penalties, doing a lot of different things. It took me a while to grasp the concepts and how the coaches wanted us to play."

What was so different about Babcock's strategy? A number of elements, of which the main one involved trusting that Canada's defensemen needed to leave their points when playing an aggressive, offensive game. "He wanted the left wings driving across, he wanted defensemen to jump into the play," Pronger said. "They wanted us to play an up-tempo game. And early on, in that process of understanding and buying in, I'm thinking, 'If I jump here, is there going to be somebody there?' If you've never played a certain system and played a certain way for the better

part of 15 years, it can be a little alarming at times with the indecision and not knowing if this is going to work out. Will I look foolish if I jump and nobody's there to support me?"

On just about any other team, Pronger would have been afforded the time and space necessary to adjust to Babcock's blueprint. Unfortunately for him, Babcock didn't have that type of time, and had excellent other options to use on defense in Duncan Keith, Drew Doughty, Scott Niedermayer and Shea Weber. As such, he wasn't at all afraid to drop Pronger down to the third pairing (usually with Dan Boyle, but occasionally with Brent Seabrook) in Canada's initial games.

That relative drop in stature unnerved and frustrated Pronger when the preliminary round began. Where he was used to logging up to 30 minutes a game in a central role, he suddenly was playing closer to half that. But he was also struggling through some off-ice family issues and admits that his mind wasn't always where it needed to be.

Still, the way the cream of the crop usually does in hockey, Pronger adapted. As Canada beat the Germans in the qualification round, then the Russians in the quarterfinal and Slovakia in the semifinal, he demonstrated to Babcock that he'd exited his comfort zone and was willing to play it the coach's way. When that gold medal game finally arrived and Pronger was assigned the task of defending against Patrick Kane, who had scored twice against Finland in the other semifinal, he was peaking at precisely the right time. He'd played just 14:05 against the U.S. in their round-robin loss to the Americans, but in the rematch he played a team-high 23:35. And the fact he held Kane to a pair of assists while seeing more game action than any Canadian that Sunday afternoon in Vancouver was thoroughly gratifying for him. "The minutes-played in the final kind of speaks for itself," Pronger said. "We were matched up against Kane's line all night, and we

> "I WAS A LITTLE BEHIND THE 8-BALL IN WHAT WE WERE TRYING TO DO, KILLING PENALTIES, DOING A LOT OF DIFFERENT THINGS. IT TOOK ME A WHILE TO GRASP THE CONCEPTS AND HOW THE COACHES WANTED US TO PLAY."

did a good job of shutting them down and not allowing them many scoring opportunities. Personally, and from a team standpoint, we played extremely well."

Despite not registering a blip on the scoresheet, Pronger values that 2010 contest more than any other because it was the culmination of a two-week professional rollercoaster ride that saw him branch out into unfamiliar areas under a new coach's style to lock down an offensive dynamo like Kane and help his teammates deliver a massive emotional uplift to the deliriously overjoyed Canadian crowd. "Personally, it was a victory in and of itself, as I was able to earn back the trust of the coaches," Pronger said. "And it's one of those things where you're on home soil, a lot of friends and family and all the Canadians cheering you on. It's pretty special being part of something like that."

BY ADAM PROTEAU

KERRY FRASER

MAY 2, 1985

QUEBEC 3 VS. MONTREAL 2

•••

Not wanting a repeat of the mayhem from the year before, Fraser didn't just have to worry about fights breaking out. The young referee had to worry about a breakout of his own.

"It transcended anything we had seen in previous rivalries. It transcended the game on the ice. It was about families. It was about business, ownership. And we felt it. Because as I stepped into that city, it took on a form like you'd never see elsewhere."
—Kerry Fraser

On a spring afternoon in 1985, Kerry Fraser stood in a Montreal pharmacy, his shirt pulled open, desperate for relief. The longtime referee, who wore stripes in the NHL for 30 years until his retirement in 2010, was just 32 years old and in his third year in the league when his body seemed to betray him.

It was the worst possible timing. Days earlier, Fraser had received a call for the assignment of a career. On May 2, he was to report to Montreal for Game 7 between the Canadiens and Nordiques. As the famed Battle of Quebec crested to its brutal finish, Fraser was tabbed to officiate.

The ferocity of the rivalry was not lost on the young ref. A year earlier, during Game 6 of the 1984 Adams division final, so volatile did the Montreal-Quebec series get that brawls spilled over from the second period straight through into warmups during the next intermission. Fraser watched fellow referee Bruce Hood lose control of the game – and some said his career, too. After 21 years on the ice, amid the wreckage in Montreal of what became known as the Good Friday Massacre, Hood retired following that year's playoffs.

Such was the context awaiting Fraser in 1985 in Quebec, where the series rematch meant much more than just hockey. The morning before the game, Fraser hopped on the earliest possible flight into Montreal from his hometown of Sarnia, Ont. He wanted to arrive early to focus and to prepare himself. Immediately upon touching down, the significance of Game 7 hit him. "Mr. Fraser," the airport baggage handler greeted him. "So nice to see you. Big game tomorrow night." The welcome continued as he stepped outside to catch a cab. "Mr. Fraser!" boomed the taxi line attendant. "Big game tomorrow night. Who's going to win?"

Fraser did all he could to calm his nerves ahead of the game. He checked into his hotel, the Sheraton Centre downtown, and spent much of the afternoon strolling through the city. He turned in not long after dinner, around 8:30 p.m., for a long rest he was sure he'd need. Fraser thought he would be ready, but overnight something inside him changed.

The next morning, game day, he awoke to a terrible feeling. "Before I even pulled the covers back," Fraser said, "I felt like my body was on fire."

Up and down, Fraser was covered in red blotches – painfully itchy raised welts that seemed to swallow him whole, from his chest down to the tops of his feet. He rushed along Blvd. René-Levesque until he found the first drugstore in sight, the blotches becoming more inflamed now, more discomforting. "They were itchy as all get-out," he said. "I just wanted to claw at myself."

Fraser hurried toward the pharmacist, an older man with grey hair and glasses sliding down his nose, by the counter in the back. Discretion was very important for the referee at this juncture. He was being recognized all over town, and although mercifully the marks had spared his hands and face, he couldn't be sure that someone in the drugstore hadn't already placed him. Nobody could be allowed to think that the man in charge of that night's cutthroat playoff game was compromised in any way.

With his back toward other customers in the store, Fraser showed his blotchy skin to the pharmacist, who took a beat before asking him if he was allergic to any food. Fraser replied that he was not. The pharmacist then asked if he was feeling nervous about anything. Fraser could hardly keep his voice down. "Uh, yeah!" he exclaimed.

The pharmacist suggested that Fraser was suffering from a bad case of hives, brought on by anxiety. He was prescribed an antihistamine, something non-drowsy, and off he went. That evening, Fraser told his fellow refs he needed to go on ahead without them to the Montreal Forum to get some equipment tended to, but that was a ruse. In fact, he just needed to go earlier than his colleagues so he could slip into his long underwear and uniform without them seeing him covered in blotches.

As the arena came to life above him, Fraser went through his pre-game exercises, itching and dying to scratch nearly every inch of his body. He had refereed games through pain and discomfort before – in 1982, for example, when Paul Coffey shattered Fraser's fibula with a slapshot minutes into a game that the ref grit through to the end – but never on this stage.

There was no longer time to think of himself. Two of the fiercest rivals in hockey were ready to decide a series. "Once I dropped the puck," Fraser said, "it was game on."

Of course it would be overtime. After 60 intense minutes, a 2-2 tie led Montreal and Quebec to an extra period to settle the series.

Fraser was still in the zone. He had no chance, nor the inclination, to think about his burning body. He had one final period to make sure was called right, to guarantee that the players, not the officials, were the ones to decide the game.

Before the Nordiques moved to Denver in 1995, there had been few rivalries like Quebec-Montreal. It was intra-provincial, but more than that, too. It seemed to create fault lines between communities, and even between businesses – the teams were owned by competing beer companies Molson and Carling O'Keefe. "Family members fist-fought over the team they supported," Fraser said.

During Game 7, the Forum had been abuzz the entire night, the tension so thick Fraser thought the building's roof would blow at any minute. "It was electric," Fraser said. "The game was a powder keg."

Then, suddenly, it happened. Two minutes into OT, Fraser saw Peter Stastny bat a rebound into the back of the net. The Habs were vanquished, the Nordiques off to the next round. Quebec fell eventually to Philadelphia, before the Flyers lost the Stanley Cup to Wayne Gretzky's Edmonton Oilers. The Nordiques never again reached the conference finals.

As soon as he watched the puck go in, Fraser exhaled. "The air went out of me with a sigh of relief," he said. Mercifully, the goal had been

> "BEFORE I EVEN PULLED THE COVERS BACK, I FELT LIKE MY BODY WAS ON FIRE."

clean, and he'd escaped the series unscathed. The young referee had earned his stripes.

Fraser skated off the Forum ice back into the referees' dressing room. It was time for the moment of truth. He took a breath and began to dis-robe, unsure what he'd find underneath. When he looked down, there was no mistaking it. "My skin," Fraser said, "was white as snow."

BY JASON BUCKLAND

MICHAEL LEIGHTON

APRIL 24, 2008

PHILADELPHIA 3 VS. ALBANY 2

• • •

In 2014, Leighton backstopped his KHL club to a quadruple overtime win – the longest game in league history. But it wasn't the first time the journeyman goaltender had set such a record while turning aside truckloads of rubber.

"We're all pros, and we all play this game to win, but I was somewhat glad it was over."
—Michael Leighton

Michael Leighton stared at the scoreboard. Sweat dripped down his face, his goalie pads felt like mattresses on his weary legs and his teammates were bent over their sticks with no gas left in the tank. He thought to himself, "Not again..."

It was spring 2014, and Leighton, a former NHL backstop, was toiling for Donbass HC, the Ukraine-based team in the KHL. It was Game 2 of the semifinal between Donbass and Lev Praha, and the teams went into overtime, about to bring new meaning to the term "extra time." It wasn't until four overtime periods expired – 126 minutes and 14 seconds – before Donbass put an end to the longest game in league history.

For Leighton, however, it was old hat.

Six years prior to that night, Leighton was part of another monumental game – the longest in AHL history. In that game, Leighton made 98 saves (another league record) as his Albany River Rats fell 3-2 to the Philadelphia Phantoms in a first-round playoff series. The game ran 142 minutes and 58 seconds over – that's five hours and 38 minutes of actual time – from the drop of the puck to the final whistle.

In addition to yet another Phantoms' record of 101 shots taken, the game also offered two unofficial firsts: the only time a goalie with 98 saves was merely a second star, and the only time a player on a losing team acknowledged he might have been happy the game was over. "To tell you the truth," Leighton said, "I was so exhausted, I was like, 'Yeah, whatever, let's get out of here.' "

That day in late April 2008 felt no different than any other for Leighton, a minor-leaguer just getting his foot in the NHL door. Following the morning skate and his afternoon nap, Leighton got to the rink and played some soccer, taped his sticks and fiddled with his equipment – the stuff he'd done before every game in his life.

But once he stepped out onto the ice, he got an indication that this night was going to be different. The Phantoms were shooting from every direction. Leighton met the challenge, though, turning aside shot after shot, controlling rebounds and watching his defense clear them away.

This, it was now evident, was going to be a good night.

Then the game went to overtime.

The first 20 minutes solved nothing. Neither did the second. "By the third overtime, it was a boring game," Leighton said. "Guys were just dumping and chasing, or trying to chase. Nobody had any energy. I was like, 'Come on, just finish this.' "

Leighton and the Phantoms' netminder, Scott Munroe, were throwing up walls in their respective creases, and their confidence grew with every save. "I felt unbeatable," Leighton said.

The game more than doubled, entering the fourth overtime. There were few left in the Times Union Center, except for the diehards, who watched Leighton foil a 2-on-0 breakaway, just hoping for an end to the madness.

The players were gulping down water and Gatorade. They couldn't get enough bananas and protein bars. Some were hooked up to IV bags during the intermissions. Down the corridor, the Phantoms were enjoying the pizza they'd ordered.

Back on the ice, the teams prepared for a fifth overtime period. Leighton watched as the shot clock climbed toward triple digits: 97... 98... 99. Then it flipped over to 00. Teammate Brett Bellemore skated toward his goaltender and tapped on the pads.

Whoever was left in the rink – by then it was about 12:30 a.m., and the concession stands had long since shut down – were chanting "MVP! MVP!" And then, on the 101st shot, Ryan Potulny

> ## "TO TELL YOU THE TRUTH. I WAS SO EXHAUSTED, I WAS LIKE, 'YEAH, WHATEVER, LET'S GET OUT OF HERE.' "

put it past Leighton to win it for the Phantoms.

Leighton fell to the ice, purely and undeniably exhausted. In the River Rats dressing room, he sat motionless at his stall for almost half an hour. "No doubt there was some disappointment," Leighton recalled. "Every hockey player wants to win every game he's in, but there weren't a lot of guys who weren't happy this one was done."

This was early Friday morning, and the River Rats had a long bus trip to look forward to later in the day. Physically and mentally drained, most of the players slept on the road to Philadelphia.

In Game 6 of the series Saturday, Leighton turned in a 40-save shutout performance. "My goals-against average and save percentage were amazing in that series," he said. Alas, the River Rats lost to the Phantoms in seven games.

Leighton would become a full-time NHLer the next two years, with the Carolina Hurricanes and Philadelphia Flyers. In the spring of 2010, he backstopped Philly to the Stanley Cup final against the Chicago Blackhawks. The most shots he faced in any one game against Chicago was 41 in Game 6, the series-clincher. He stopped 37 of them.

BY ROBIN SHORT

ANDRÉ SAVARD

FEBRUARY 5, 1971

QUEBEC 14 VS. ROSEMONT 1

•••

Twelve points in a game is an impressive feat, to say the least.
Did Savard do it for glory? To catch the eye of scouts? Nope.
He did it so his linemate Lafleur wouldn't prank him after the game.

"If Guy Lafleur had one goal, he wanted two. If he had two, he wanted three.
Some guys, they have two goals and they won't press on the pedal as much.
But we had good chemistry on our line. We had the same attitude. You keep going right
from the drop of the puck until the end. You keep going. Part of the game is you've got
to win. It's nice to participate and get some points."
—André Savard

Their dressing room stalls were adjacent, nestled in the bowels of the famed Colisée de Quebec. André Savard and Guy Lafleur, two parts of the most powerful line in the QMJHL, sat beside each other before every game.

Savard, who was in the midst of his second season as a center with the Quebec Remparts, looked up to his 19-year-old right winger because of the immense talent that would make him a Hall of Famer. Their relationship was like that of brothers. Of course, since Lafleur was older, life was sometimes difficult for Savard. Lafleur's regular prank was stealing the towel from Savard's stall. Players only had the right to one towel, so the younger would either have to find it or plead with the trainer to give him a new one. The pranks in this spirit were mostly in good fun. "There was only one guy that got away with that," Savard said, "and that was him."

An outstanding performance against the Rosemont National, Savard figured, would save him a post-game scavenger hunt. That meant keeping up with – and even outdoing – whatever Lafleur had to offer.

Savard always made sure to study Lafleur's approach, the approach of a player who would eventually lead the league in scoring with 209 points. Lafleur's steeliness was something Savard had noted before. On this February night, Lafleur was particularly quiet and focused. His determination was apparent. "He was my winger, so obviously I had to take advantage of that," Savard said. "I wanted extra points all the time."

The Remparts were a major junior powerhouse. They would go on to win the President's Cup that season – one of three in the four years Savard played on the team – and also claimed the Memorial Cup. They lost just seven times in 62 regular season games.

Fans at the Colisée ate it up. The arena was regularly filled almost to capacity, and the building was always loud. On this night, 8,693 spectators packed the place in expectation of a decisive win over Rosemont, the team that was placed second-to-last.

And the QMJHL's top line pounced. Savard racked up seven first-period assists on five goals from Lafleur and a pair from left winger Michel Briere. The three players were the top scorers in the QMJHL that season. Briere had 144 points, while Savard finished third, five points back.

It was like clockwork against Rosemont. "The three of us had a certain level of talent, Lafleur being the best," Savard said. "He was easy to find because he stayed on his wing."

The outcome was a drubbing, a 14-1 Quebec win. Savard rounded out his hat trick with 3:04 to play, collecting his 12th point. It was one more than Lafleur and two more than Briere.

> ## "THE THREE OF US HAD A CERTAIN LEVEL OF TALENT, LAFLEUR BEING THE BEST. HE WAS EASY TO FIND BECAUSE HE STAYED ON HIS WING."

It was also a CHL record. "It's something you've got to be proud about," Savard said. "We worked to get that."

Savard has seen his share of special offensive performances. He was drafted sixth overall by the Boston Bruins in 1973 and was an opponent during Darryl Sittler's 10-point NHL game with Toronto. Others have come close to equalling Savard's CHL mark. Most recently, fellow Rempart Alexander Radulov recorded 11 points in a March 2006 outing.

Savard, now 63, is a pro scout for the New Jersey Devils. He divides his time between Florida and Quebec City, where he manages to watch his share of QMJHL action. Because of the way coaches pre-scout using video, he assumes his record is safe. "It would be hard to break, that's for sure," he said.

Back in 1971, Savard didn't even know he had set a new high-water mark until the next day. After the game, he spent the 25-minute walk back to his billets' house thinking about his remarkable feat. As soon as he got home, he called his mother, Dolorese, in Témiscaming, Que. Because she only got television and radio stations from North Bay, Ont., she had no idea of her son's exploits 500 miles away. "I don't know if it sank in," Savard said. "She was certainly happy."

Savard was happy, too. He got his record – and his towel was right where he left it.

BY DANIEL NUGENT-BOWMAN

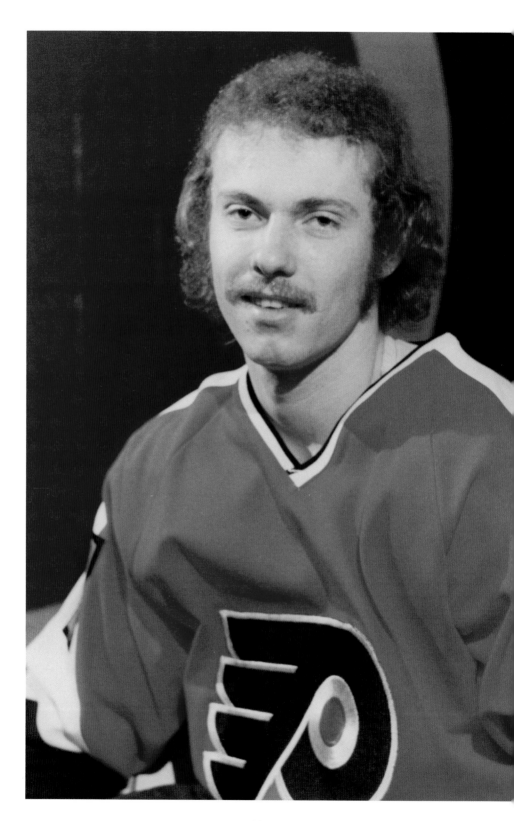

AL HILL

 ## PHILADELPHIA 6 VS. ST. LOUIS 4

•••

As an undrafted 21-year-old making his NHL debut, Hill was desperate to make a big impression on the veteran Broad Street Bullies. And he did just that, scoring during his first shift on his way to setting an NHL rookie record that still stands today.

"I'm not going to resent the fact that I've got it, that everybody you do see remembers that one game. It would be nice if they would say, 'You were a good checking forward and a dependable player.' It was a lucky game, and everything just went my way."
—Al Hill

H e knew it was going to be Mission Improbable. How was a 21-year-old kid, an undrafted talent from faraway B.C., supposed to crack the Philadelphia boys' club of the Broad Street Bullies without so much as a morning skate to get his bearings?

To top it off, Al Hill almost didn't even make it to the game of his life. His call-up to the Philadelphia Flyers for the fateful 1977 Valentine's Day home skirmish against the St. Louis Blues was a test of will from the outset. Playing for the AHL Springfield Indians, Hill's bus didn't get home from a Feb. 13 game at Rochester until 4:30 a.m. that day.

His head had barely hit the pillow when the phone rang. "Get going to Philly right away," commanded the voice. "Bill Barber is injured and they need you tonight." Only one more problem: a big snowstorm. It took Hill all day to get to the City of Brotherly Love, and he arrived there only to find he would be starting the game on the first shift with future Hall of Famer Bobby Clarke and a guy they called 'The Hound' – Bob Kelly – at the sold-out, raucous Spectrum.

Talk about pressure. Some people don't take well to it, but others, like Hill, thrive under it. He needed only 36 seconds to score his first NHL goal against goaltender Yves Belanger, prompting fans to turn and look at each other asking, "Who is this guy?"

Almost 10 minutes later, Hill scored another goal, cementing his monosyllabic name in the memory of the Flyers' fan base. A string of assists followed, along with a fight, no less, to create a Gordie Howe hat trick for the ages.

Hill said that NHL record debut performance in the Flyers' 6-4 win may not have been his most technically sound game, but agrees that the five-point night was his most important, getting him through the door of that exclusive two-time Stanley Cup fraternity and starting the journeyman on an on-and-off eight-year NHL career. "It was tough because they were so close-knit, you know," Hill said. "They won two Stanley Cups (1974, 1975) and the third year (1976) they lost in the final. All of a sudden I come in, and it wasn't an easy team to crack."

One thing working in Hill's favor was his versatility. No doubt his 172 penalty minutes with the WHL Victoria Cougars in 1975-76 had caught the eyes of both Flyers GM Keith Allen and coach Fred 'The Fog' Shero. Plus, Hill could kill penalties and even take the odd shift on the power play.

Still, anytime there was a new kid in town, the veterans kept a sharp eye to make sure the young stranger had the right stuff. "Yeah, I'm sure it raised a few eyebrows," Hill said. "But I knew I still had a lot of work to do. I knew I wasn't going to stay up. I knew I still had to go back down to the AHL and hone my skills a little bit."

And that's exactly what happened. After that legendary effort, Hill stayed only eight more games with the Flyers that season and registered just a solitary assist. And so began a rollercoaster NHL career that would see him play a mere 221 games until his retirement following the 1988-89 campaign.

To this day, people ask Hill, now 60 and a pro scout with the Flyers, if he somehow resents the fact that he's best remembered for one game and not for achievements like his 16 goals in the 1979-80 season when the Flyers set a professional sports record 35-game (25-0-10) unbeaten streak. Hill shakes his head. Every Valentine's Day, his two sons call him on the phone to reminisce about the performance. After all, it was a magical night when everything went right.

BY WAYNE FISH

MICK VUKOTA

OCTOBER 20, 1989

NEW YORK 5 VS. WASHINGTON 3

•••

As a prototypical 1980s tough guy, Vukota was better known for sitting in the sin bin for five minutes at a time. But after a pep talk from his team's star sniper, his five minutes of fame came while he was actually on the ice.

"My teammates were so happy for me – that's what I remember most from that night. A lot of nights, you're out there banging away, trying to help the team by fighting and doing whatever is needed. But to chip in offensively and have the guys appreciate it really made that night memorable, more than anything."
—Mick Vukota

Marinko 'Mick' Vukota spent much of the team bus ride to Landover, Md. on Oct. 20, 1989 lost in thought. He wasn't focused on that night's game against a Patrick Division rival. Instead, he'd given in to worrying about when he'd finally start contributing to the New York Islanders in ways other than throwing punches and racking up penalty minutes.

Vukota had been feeling increasingly down about himself since the start of the season two weeks earlier. He wasn't getting consistent ice time, and he was questioning his value to an Islanders club that had missed the playoffs for the first time in 14 years the previous season. The regular shift he used to log in junior and the minors was all but forgotten, and Vukota was starting to think it might never come back. The gnawing sense that he didn't belong on New York's roster was worsened by the thought of that night's opponent.

The Washington Capitals had been the only NHL club to invite the undrafted Vukota to train-

ing camp on a tryout basis, but they eventually cut ties with him and later turned down the chance to make him a counteroffer when the Islanders came calling. "I don't know if I was pouting, but it was obvious that something was bothering me because Pat LaFontaine pulled me aside on the bus and asked me to sit with him," Vukota said. "He said, 'Make sure you understand that your role is just as important as my role on this team. I have to do my job and you're doing your job. It's as important as mine.' "

Vukota disembarked from the bus at Capital Centre feeling inspired. His worry had subsided, washed away in the wake of LaFontaine's impromptu motivational speech. But Vukota had no idea of just how impactful that pep talk from the team's scoring leader would be until he hit the ice.

Aside from his chat with LaFontaine, everything went as it always did before a game. Vukota didn't change any of his routines: He grabbed the same stick, applied the same tape job and warmed up the same way he always did (though with a little extra energy, admittedly), skating across from the team that had sent him home from camp not long before.

The game started normally enough, until the first-period goals started coming, all of them from the most unlikely of sources. Vukota netted his first at 10:08, kicking the puck to his stick and snapping home a shot from the low slot. His second came at 14:40, as he forced a turnover in front of the net and swept a juicy rebound into an empty net. "After that goal, we lined up for the faceoff, and to be honest with you, I was expecting Washington to send somebody out to fight," Vukota said. "We were up 2-0 on the road, and it was me, of all people, causing the mayhem."

> ## "AFTER THAT GOAL, WE LINED UP FOR THE FACEOFF, AND TO BE HONEST WITH YOU, I WAS EXPECTING WASHINGTON TO SEND SOMEBODY OUT TO FIGHT."

The Capitals opted not to send him a message on the next shift, though. Instead, Vukota sent them another one of his own. Driving to the net off the rush, he poked home a loose puck and completed his natural hat trick at 15:08 of the opening period, capping a five-minute scoring spree that staked the Islanders to a 3-0 lead.

Emerging from the crush of his linemates in the far corner, Vukota slowly skated back to the bench, breaking into a smile even bigger than the ones he wore on each of his two previous return trips. There he spotted LaFontaine waiting to congratulate him just outside the bench door, with a smile just as big as Vukota's.

BY MICHAEL WILLHOFT

MIKE RICHTER

UNITED STATES 5 VS. CANADA 2

•••

Sixteen years after the Miracle on Ice, Richter almost singlehandedly led the United States to a gold medal as the underdogs at the inaugural World Cup of Hockey, upsetting Canada right in its own backyard.

*"It had been a long time since 1980. We were a new generation
of Americans who wanted to prove we could compete at this level."
—Mike Richter*

Mike Richter knew the pressure would be overwhelming. Playing in the NHL for the New York Rangers had its own measure of pressure, but representing your country in the first World Cup of Hockey in 1996 would be another level. Yet the Pennsylvania-born goaltender welcomed it. "I just felt like if I went out there and played my best, things would fall into place," Richter said. "These tournaments are all-star games, and whoever is playing well at the time wins."

Richter had won a Stanley Cup with the Rangers two years earlier, but Game 3 of the World Cup final is the greatest game he ever played. His performance earned him most valuable player of the tournament.

Not yet 30, Richter remembers having his summer end prematurely and joining a group of American-born teammates in Providence, R.I., for a short training camp prior to a tournament most felt would be won by Canada. The challenge of upsetting the Canadians motivated Richter, who beat out Guy Hebert and Jim Carey to become the United States' starter in net, but it was the jovial atmosphere throughout the World

Cup that he remembers best. "It was a group of guys who were so funny you never wanted to leave," Richter said. "We'd laugh our butts off at every team meal. I was lucky to have Brian Leetch there from the Rangers. He was a good friend. And Billy Guerin and Keith Tkachuk were always coming up with something. Real entertainment. We were very serious once the game got going, but we had a real lightness and a jump in our step as a team."

They would need more than that to defeat Canada in the best-of-three final, particularly after losing to their rivals in overtime for Game 1 at Philadelphia on Sept. 10. Steve Yzerman skated down the wing in OT and took what Richter called a "fade-away jumper" before shooting the puck back across the grain through a screen. The U.S. goaltender couldn't stop it, and Canada moved to one victory away from winning it all.

Although the tournament moved to Montreal for the second and third games, Richter and his teammates actually felt some of the pressure decrease. They knew they could contend with the powerful Canadian team, and playing on home ice would raise the pressure level for Canada. Indeed, a 5-2 U.S. victory in Game 2 set up a winner-take-all finale on Sept. 14.

Richter didn't have any glaring superstitions, so his plan was simply to fall into his normal routine the day and night before the final game. After a practice, which he recalled was attended by a horde of media, he made sure his equipment was in order and went back to the hotel to relax and wait. He watched a movie, did some reading and made some calls to friends and family before the team meal at the hotel.

He had a confident calmness on the day of the final game, but that was shattered when Canada immediately took control. Suddenly, Richter felt under siege. "The Canadians were on their toes and were putting everything on the net," he said. "That's what they did well. Throw it at the net, crash, get screens and work hard. They were outshooting us. I had a lot of work."

Richter kept the game scoreless with magnificent goaltending, and it was impressive. If the U.S. was somehow to win this game, Richter had to be at the top of the list of most MVP voters. But Team Canada had other ideas. "I remember toward the end of the second period we were up maybe 1-0, and Eric Lindros tipped one in the last minute or two," Richter said. "I was really disappointed. We wanted to keep them frustrated going into the third period. That goal gave

> ## "THE CANADIANS WERE ON THEIR TOES AND WERE PUTTING EVERYTHING ON THE NET."

them some life. You never want to give up a goal late."

At 12:50 of the third period, Adam Foote wristed a shot from the point that Richter never saw to give Canada a 2-1 lead. Richter knew he couldn't allow another goal, and he didn't. Vincent Damphousse had a breakaway and had Richter going the wrong way with one of his moves, but somehow the goalie reached back and put his stick across the front of the open net to make the save and spoil the breakaway. Scott Niedermayer skated in from the point and fired a shot that seemed certain to go in, but Richter made the stop. And the saves kept coming.

Inspired by their goaltender, the Americans scored four goals in the final few minutes to come back and win it 5-2. It would be a game Richter would never forget. And, in a sense, it would put his name alongside an earlier group of Americans. Richter was 13 years old when the U.S. upset the Soviet Union in the 1980 Olympics at Lake Placid, N.Y. The 1996 team wasn't quite the underdog that the Miracle on Ice squad was, but it was a fight right to the end. "I knew we had a very good team," Richter said. "But you also have to be aware that you're in a very good tournament, and no team is going to roll over and die for you."

BY RICH CHERE

DARRYL SITTLER

FEBRUARY 7, 1976

TORONTO 11 vs. BOSTON 4

●●●

Some records just aren't meant to be broken. Forty years later, Sittler's mark of 10 points in a single game has withstood the test of time.

"People say, 'Hey, that record is never going to be broken.' I hope it doesn't get broken, but if it does, I could understand why, because that's sports. The unknown can happen to anybody, as it did to me, so I'd respect that. And if it did happen, well, good on the guy that did it."
—Darryl Sittler

Staring across a table at 65-year-old Darryl Sittler, you'd never guess he accomplished his most famous feat four decades ago. His posture is perfect. He has the firm handshake of a man who still works out at his local gym at least three times a week. He oozes a quiet, classy confidence. He could strut around like he owns the place, but he chooses modesty instead.

Sittler sits in the THN office, eyes glued to the pages of a February 1976 edition like it's a pulpy novel he can't put down. After a quick dig through the archives, we've unearthed the newsprint cover detailing his signature NHL accomplishment.

It's a record so astounding it feels pulled from a video game or a movie, but it's all too real. Everything clicked for Sittler on Feb. 7, 1976, when his Toronto Maple Leafs hosted the Boston Bruins. Maurice Richard's single-game record of eight points stood for 32 years and 9,453 NHL games before Sittler smashed it with a 10-pointer that night.

The natural question to ask when the stars align so perfectly, producing a stat line so astro-

nomical, is what put the player in the physical or mental state to pull it off? Nothing seemed out of the ordinary for Sittler on the ice leading up to the game. He was in the midst of a solid season for the Maple Leafs but wasn't threatening league scoring leader Guy Lafleur of the Habs. Sittler's Leafs were struggling on the brink of the Adams Division playoff picture with a 21-20-11 record, and they only had one win in their previous eight games. He didn't feel anything epic on the horizon, especially with the piping-hot Bruins approaching on the schedule. "Players don't look at it that way," he said. "You just approach every game with the mentality that, hey, you're going to be prepared, you're going to do the best you can. We had some good, young players like Lanny McDonald coming up. Borje Salming was coming into his own. Ian Turnbull. So we were going to have a good team, all in their early 20s. At that time, I was only 25. So you're hopeful."

The Saturday night game had some emotion fuelling it, however. Sittler always noticed an extra buzz in the air when he and the fans in attendance knew it was *Hockey Night in Canada* on CBC. And Leafs owner Harold Ballard had thrown down the gauntlet a few days earlier, wishing loudly in the press that he had a center to play with McDonald and Dave 'Tiger' Williams. "Obviously, it was a bit of a shot toward me," Sittler said. "But that was Harold, you know? And then, that night, everything just fell into place and happened. Did that motivate me any more or any less? No. I always approached every game with the same mentality."

Sittler insists he played with no chip on his shoulder, but did Ballard's words have an unconscious effect? We have no way of knowing. What we do know is Sittler's off-ice routine completely changed on Feb. 7. Professional hockey players are creatures of habit. Game days include morning skates, often a midday nap and, for most, the same pre-game meal each time. Sittler took his morning skate at Maple Leaf Gardens, but the rest of his day didn't follow the usual pattern.

Sittler's wife, Wendy, typically made him an afternoon meal before his nap. But she had somewhere to be that day. Sittler was left to his own devices and got caught downtown. The nap was a must, so he decided to grab some takeout and eat it on the way home. His choice: Swiss Chalet roast chicken and fries. "I was eating it while it was still hot, off the front seat of my car," he said. "And then you go out and get 10 points, and you ask, 'What are the things you did differently?' That was one of the things."

Sittler, belly full of fast food, arrived at Maple Leaf Gardens to tangle with the Bruins in front of 16,385 fans. Boston's star-crossed goalie that evening: rookie Dave Reece, about to be sent back to the minors with Gerry Cheevers returning from the World Hockey Association. Game on.

Things started familiarly enough 6:19 into the first period, with Sittler, a deft playmaker, springing his triggerman McDonald, who gained the Boston zone and beat Reece from the top of the

> ## "YOU GO OUT AND GET 10 POINTS, AND YOU ASK, 'WHAT ARE THE THINGS YOU DID DIFFERENTLY?' "

circle. "Lanny and I were in sync," Sittler said. "Sometimes, you get the chance to play with players that you have that instinctive intuitiveness of where they're going to be, where to pass it, and all that stuff. Few players you get that with, but Lanny and I had that."

Less than a minute later, Sittler narrowly avoided a hit from stud Bruins blueliner Brad Park and set Turnbull up for a heavy slapshot, solving an aggressive Reece. Two points for Sittler, but it was very much business as usual at that point. "I don't even remember what the score was at the end of the first," he said.

The Leafs led Boston 2-1 after one period. Sittler joined the goal parade 2:56 into the second with an easy redirection after Salming feathered the puck onto Sittler's stick in the slot. "It was Borje that created the offense, to get me the opportunity to go to the front of the net," Sittler said. "When you look at the five guys on the ice – myself, Lanny, Errol Thompson, Borje and Ian – we were five offense-minded players, a line, a unit."

Three goals in about 23 minutes weren't enough to chase Reece from the net. Bruins coach Don Cherry didn't flinch. And Reece had no idea that the onslaught was just getting started. It resumed just 37 seconds later, on a set play, with Sittler winning the draw directly to Salming, who buried a slapshot.

Sittler's fifth point and second goal came roughly five minutes afterward, and by this point it started to feel like he and his stick could do no wrong. His seemingly harmless snapper had eyes and found its way through a Bruins defender and past a hapless Reece, who, to his credit, never wanted to be hooked from the game. Halfway to 10, Sittler already felt euphoric, since five points is a great game for anyone.

But he still didn't have the single-game record on his mind, not even when he completed the hat trick at 10:27 of the second with a one-timer on a feed in the slot from Jack Valiquette. Sittler scored point No. 6 a little more than halfway through the game, and by the time he got No. 7, assisting on Salming's second goal, he felt sorry for Reece. "A lot of those goals, Reece – he didn't have a chance on them much," Sittler said. "You can't blame him as much as saying he had a bad game. There were a lot of good goals, just inside the post. He wasn't getting a whole lot of protection out there."

The Leafs led 8-4 after 40 minutes. At this point, Sittler couldn't ignore that something special was happening. He had three goals and four assists. Team statistician Stan Obodiac excitedly hustled down to the Leafs' dressing room from the press lounge during the intermission. He told Sittler he needed one more point to equal Rocket Richard's record. Sittler's heart started drumming to a faster beat. "When you're having a good game, you're playing an Original Six team, it's in the Gardens, the building's excited, you're ahead and that in itself is exciting," he said. "But then,

starting the third period, I knew there was a shot at tying a record."

With the stakes raised, a different Sittler seemed to take the ice in the third – an even more possessed version, if that were possible. It took just 44 seconds for him to find twine again, and he did it in scintillating fashion. Salming fed him at the Boston blue line. Sittler beat Darryl Edestrand to the outside, deked left and found the far corner of the net. "That was the prettiest goal," Sittler said. "I came around the defenseman on my off side. I had lots of speed, and it's hard to defend when you're backing up and the forward's got a little bit more speed on you. When you're on your off side, you can bring the puck to your forehand, which I did there, and I tucked it inside the post. Because of the speed and the way the goal ended up, I ended up behind the net, hitting the boards and knowing at that point – that was the eighth, right? – that I had tied the record. That one was extra special."

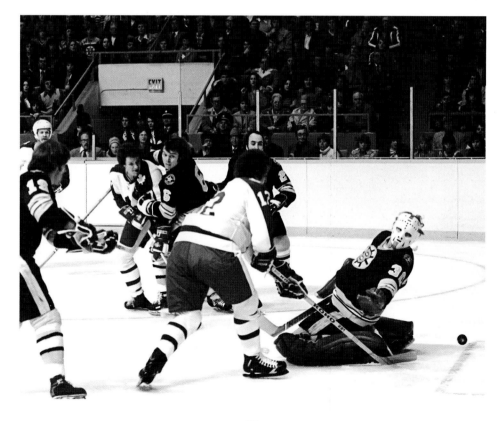

Half a period later, Sittler found the net a fifth time, twirling on his skates in elation. He'd done it. Nine points. A 32-year-old record was no more. It was a blur for the center, who, 40 years later, still can't describe what he felt. He remembers his teammates mobbing him, happy for him, but he's still at a loss when he recalls the immediate personal magnitude of what he'd done.

Sittler's sixth goal and 10th point arrived at 16:35 of the third. He could only raise his hands and shake his head. His pass ricocheted off Park and into the Bruins net. The single-game standard was set. "That one was unreal," Sittler said. "It kind of told the story. It was just one of those nights. Hey, the puck had eyes. It went in."

It's fun to picture a romanticized tale of wild celebration and partying after the win. When you play for the Leafs and get 10 points in a game, you're pretty much mayor for a night. But it wasn't that simple for Sittler. He appeared on *Hockey Night in Canada* for an interview, his teammates were thrilled and he described the night as "a friggin' fantasy land," but business had to continue, as the Leafs had a home game the next night. So the post-game bash that fateful Saturday consisted of ribs at Bobby Rubino's in Mississauga followed by a good night's sleep.

Ballard and the Leafs did formally honor Sittler a month later with a presentation at center ice in the Gardens. He received a tea service and a silver platter with the record inscribed and Ballard's signature. It remains a Sittler family heirloom.

Feb. 7, 2016 marked 40 years and 38,995 NHL games since Sittler made history. No player has matched the record. Heck, no player has even tallied nine points. Nine have recorded eight points in a game since 1976: Tom Bladon (1977), Bryan Trottier (1978), Peter and Anton Stastny (1981), Wayne Gretzky (1983, 1984), Paul Coffey (1986), Patrik Sundstrom (1988), Mario Lemieux (1988, 1988, 1989) and Sam Gagner (2012). "I often said when I was watching Wayne Gretzky get 200-plus points a season and Mario Lemieux, the skill level those guys had, that they would be the guys that would have a shot at the record," Sittler said. "If you would have said 10 years ago, 'Who would be a guy who would score eight or 10 points?' you wouldn't say Sam Gagner. But he had one of those nights. Everything went in for him. That can happen again to somebody else. It doesn't have to be Alex Ovechkin or Patrick Kane. But it could happen. It happened to me."

BY MATT LARKIN

NATIONAL HOCKEY LEAGUE

SCORE SHEET

NOTE:—Official Scorers.—Be particular to give credit for assists.

BOSTON .... 4 .... at .... *TORONTO* 11

VISITORS   SCORE   HOME TEAM   SCORE

Date .... *FEB. 7, 1976* ....   N.H.L. GAME # 479

CLUB	SCORER	ASSISTANT SCORER		TIME	VISITING TEAM	HOME TEAM
1st PERIOD						
TORONTO	McDONALD	SITTLER		6 19	F	6	6
TORONTO	TURNBULL	SITTLER	THOMPSON	7 01	I	6	6
BOSTON	RATELLE	SCHMAUTZ		16 54	P	6	6
2nd PERIOD						
TORONTO	SITTLER	SALMING	McDONALD	2 56	I	6	6
TORONTO	SALMING	SITTLER		3 33		5	6
BOSTON	SCHMAUTZ	BUCYK	RATELLE	5 19		6	6
TORONTO	SITTLER			8 12		6	6
ORONTO	SITTLER	VALIQUETTE	FERGUSON	10 27		5	6
BOSTON	BUCYK	RATELLE	SCHMAUTZ	11 06		6	6
TORONTO	FERGUSON	HAMMARSTROM	GARLAND	11 40		6	6
TORONTO	SALMING	McDONALD	SITTLER	13 57		6	6
BOSTON	RATELLE	SCHMAUTZ	BUCYK	14 35		6	6
3rd PERIOD						
TORONTO	SITTLER	SALMING	THOMPSON	0 44		5	6
TORONTO	SITTLER	THOMPSON		9 27		6	6
TORONTO	SITTLER	McDONALD		16 35		6	6

JIM HARRISON

JANUARY 30, 1973

ALBERTA 11 VS. NEW YORK 3

• • •

Before Sittler, there was Harrison. Yet with no TV footage from the night, and Harrison's memory of it fading, pro hockey's original 10-point game has been all but forgotten.

"It was the best year of my hockey career and one of those games when everything came together. I had just left Toronto and the NHL and went to the WHA and Edmonton. I was playing 30 to 40 minutes a game some nights. You're bound to improve. It just came natural. I was scoring goal after goal."
—Jim Harrison

A sk Jim Harrison about what he remembers from that one exceptional "game for the ages" many decades ago and he gets a little playful with his answer. "You mean that time we were playing the Regina Pats at home, don't you?"

Ah, no.

"We were down two goals with half a minute left. I scored three goals in 24 seconds and the last one came with four seconds left in the game. We won 6-5 against a very, very good Regina team. The home fans (in Estevan) went nuts."

Did that really happen? That's pretty darned special, come to think of it. It happened almost 50 years ago in the Western Canada League, precursor to the WHL. "I remember every detail of that last minute," Harrison said. "My linemates were Gregg Sheppard and Grant Erickson, and I also played with them in the NHL. Anyway, that's not the game you want to talk about, is it?"

No, it's not.

The real, exceptional game for the ages came six years later in the World Hockey Association

when the Alberta Oilers were hosting the New York Raiders at Edmonton Gardens on Jan. 30, 1973. Harrison did a Darryl Sittler three years before Sittler pulled the famous Darryl Sittler.

Ten points in one game. A pro hockey record. Heck, probably a record at any level of organized hockey.

Sadly, that WHA game wasn't televised, so there's no YouTube video of Harrison's 10 points that will survive the ages. While the hockey world goes gaga every decade when the Sittler 10-point NHL game hits a chronological milestone – it turned 40 years old early in 2016 – the memories of Harrison's feat are gradually fading into a blur, even in the mind of the guy who pulled it off that night. "The game was on radio, I know that," Harrison said. "And every now and then someone will come up to me and say they were at that game. That's how it will be remembered, I guess."

Harrison opened the scoring at 4:48 of the first period, then assisted on Val Fonteyne's goal 52 seconds later. When Al Hamilton scored at

11:05, Harrison got an assist and the Oilers were up 3-1 after 20 minutes.

Ask Harrison about details from that game and he mostly draws a blank. "You don't realize what you're doing at the time," he said. "You're too caught up in the emotions of the game, and those emotions don't really become distinct memories."

In the second period, Harrison drew an assist on a goal by Bob Wall at 13:25 to make it 4-2 Alberta. Harrison then got his second of the game to make it 5-2 at 15:38. Five points after 40 minutes.

In the dressing room between periods, however, Harrison's teammates weren't making a huge deal about it. "Nobody said, 'You're going for a record,' but… yeah, we knew what was going on," Harrison said. "I was on every power play."

At 25, Harrison was near the peak of a career almost evenly split between the NHL and WHA. In the NHL with Boston, Toronto and Chicago, he was mostly a third-liner with decent hands, a modicum of grit, but not much speed. In the WHA with the Oilers and Cleveland, Harrison was a top-six forward with some flash and good hockey sense.

In the third period that winter day in Northern Alberta, Harrison drew the first assist on goals by Steve Carlyle at 5:06 and Bernie Blanchette at 7:43 to give him seven points. When Rusty Patenaude scored from Ken Baird at 10:48 to put the Oilers ahead 8-2, it marked the game's only Alberta goal that Harrison wasn't in on. Harrison had assists on Doug Barrie's goal at 11:40 and Carlyle's at 12:00 to give him nine points. Then, 33 seconds later, Harrison completed the hat trick for his 10th point. Ask him about that last goal and he couldn't tell you if it was bar-down or in off his butt. "But I do remember having four or five breakaways that game and not scoring," he said.

The rival WHA considered itself a major league on par, or at least competitive with, the NHL. Only two players in the history of the NHL had ever

had eight points in a game at that point in time: Maurice Richard in 1944 and Bert Olmstead in 1954. "We knew it was one of those nights," Harrison said. "I was on the ice all the time. I probably played 30 to 40 minutes that game."

Alberta won 11-3, and the Harrison 10-pointer was big news, though mostly just in Edmonton. It was a West Coast game, and continental interest in the WHA was a fraction of that in the NHL. No sports networks and no TV coverage meant the news of Harrison's night didn't register much more than agate type in the Eastern newspapers the next morning. But the news eventually spread. "We had a game in New York not long afterward," Harrison said. "I remember as the bus pulled up I saw my name stretched across the ticket board outside Madison Square Garden: It said, 'Jim Harrison and the Alberta Oilers in town today.' That was a real thrill, seeing that."

Then, later in 1973, Harrison was told his 10-point feat was a finalist for the Wilkinson Sword Award, the award for the biggest sporting achievement of the year. "The ceremony was in Buffalo, but I ended up being runner-up to Larry Csonka and the Miami Dolphins, who had had an undefeated season in the NFL."

It was then that Harrison realized what he had done was a big deal. "That's when the hype came, that's when it really sunk in," he said. "I was in contact with a lot of American writers after that. No one had scored 10 points in a game before. It even made the Guinness Book of World Records. And that was quite an honor, to be considered for that Sword award."

Coincidentally, hockey's 10-point men, Harrison and Sittler, were good friends in the 1970s. They played together for two seasons with the Maple Leafs and often went up to the Northwest Territories in the off-season for fishing trips with Bobby Orr.

While Sittler likes to tell the story of how his pre-game meal just before his 10-point game consisted of a Swiss Chalet quarter-chicken meal

> "NOBODY SAID, 'YOU'RE GOING FOR A RECORD,' BUT…YEAH, WE KNEW WHAT WAS GOING ON. I WAS ON EVERY POWER PLAY."

deal eaten off the passenger seat in his car, Harrison doesn't recollect any of those sorts of details about what he did prior to that big game in 1973. "I always had a steak at about noon or 1 p.m., which is probably not the thing to have nowadays," he said. "Then, after the game, I went out and had some rum with my good friend Merlyn Carter, a bush pilot who ran that fishing camp up in the Territories. He kept telling me he had just witnessed the biggest thrill of his lifetime and kept buying me rum."

Now 68 and running a fishing camp near Greenwood, B.C. with his wife Caroline, Harrison lives a peaceful existence and likes to winter in nearby Grand Forks, B.C. "I wish I could tell you more details about what happened in that game, but I don't remember," he said. "I did keep the stick from that game, though. And I have a photo of me celebrating."

BY BRIAN COSTELLO

BRUCE BOUDREAU

MAY 9, 1975

TORONTO 10 VS. SHERBROOKE 4

● ● ●

Before he was leading a team behind the bench, Boudreau was leading one on the ice. But he didn't just wear the 'C' for his Memorial Cup-winning Toronto Marlboros. He led by example, scoring a record five goals in the 1975 semifinal.

"I'd go, 'Holy crap! Another one, another one, another one.' It was pretty cool."
—Bruce Boudreau

In 1973, Bruce Boudreau was one of the few 18-year-olds on the Toronto Marlboros that claimed the championship that every team in the Canadian major junior system dreams to call theirs. The Memorial Cup was back in the big city and a five-year drought – an eternity for this franchise – was over. It was in its rightful place.

After all, this was the team you wanted to be on as a youth playing in the Greater Toronto area. If you starred for the Marlies – the nickname most used to refer to the team – then maybe, just maybe, you might one day play for the Maple Leafs. Every boy's dream. And Boudreau was in the process of living that, a big man at school even if he wasn't one in the physical sense. "People knew the Marlies almost as well as the Leafs," Boudreau said. "Going to school... everybody knew who you were. You were a celebrity back then. To be a Marlie was pretty impressive."

Two years later, the Marlboros were his team. Four stars from the 1973 squad – Mark Howe, Wayne Dillon, Peter Marrin and Tom Edur – had signed on with the World Hockey Association, and their loss was greatly felt. Not yet 20,

Boudreau was now the Marlies' star and their captain.

John Tonelli, who would go on to become a main cog in the New York Islanders' dynasty, had quit the team right before the Ontario Major Junior Hockey League playoffs so that his status in the WHA wouldn't be jeopardized. Still, Toronto had plenty of firepower in Boudreau, John Anderson and Mark Napier, who would be a two-time 40-goal scorer with Montreal.

The night before they were to take on the Sherbrooke Castors in the Memorial Cup semifinal at Kitchener Memorial Auditorium, Boudreau and Napier, his roommate for the tournament, were up late, perhaps later than they should have been. But they had reason to be confident. After all, the Marlies opened the tournament with a 5-4 overtime win against them. "They were all French," Boudreau said. "In the Quebec League they scored a lot, so you looked at their numbers. 'Oh, these guys are really good.' And then we kicked their ass."

They had reasons to be cocksure. The Marlies had been pushed to the limit in the OMJHL playoffs by the Kingston Canadians, Sudbury Wolves and Hamilton Fincups but still emerged as the league's champion. Sure, there had been Sherbrooke, king of the QMJHL, and this tough outfit out of the WHL, the New Westminster Bruins, but the Marlies had battled valiantly thus far.

In Boudreau's mind, their toughest tests were behind them. "The Memorial Cup was sort of a cakewalk," he said. "I can't recall us being really nervous. We wanted to play good because we knew scouts were there. That was the big thing."

May 9, 1975 would become a day that would go down in history. Any doubt about the rematch with Sherbrooke was dispelled in the first period as Toronto jumped out with a big lead and was never threatened. Boudreau scored. And scored. And scored. And scored. And scored.

With five goals, the Marlies won 10-4. But that night was about the kid from northern Toronto. No player had done that in more than the five decades of Memorial Cup history, and none has matched that feat in the 40 years since.

How does a night like that come about? A combination of things. Sherbrooke's players were making regular visits to the penalty box, and Boudreau was an offensive savant in his third junior season, capturing the Eddie Powers Memorial Trophy as the OMJHL's top scorer with 165 points. His 68 goals were tied for top in the league with Peter Lee of the Ottawa 67's.

Give the top offensive player on a team of scorers some power plays and you can guess what will happen. "I'm sure they took way more penalties than they wanted to," Boudreau said. "We were a small, fast team, and it was the first game of the Memorial Cup final, too, so maybe the refs were trying to do something. We didn't have a highly penalized team. We had nobody tough. Mike Kitchen, who's an assistant coach in

Chicago, is 5-foot-10, and he was our toughest guy. But what we did have was some dynamic scoring talent."

Boudreau cleaned up on the man advantage. All five goals came that way, and they were "easy plays," as he recalled, tap-ins or rebounds that were put away.

Buoyed by the rousing semifinal, the Marlboros faced New Westminster for the championship. Coach George Armstrong had built his players back up after a round-robin loss to the Bruins, which had a future star in Stan Smyl and ruffians in Barry Beck, Clayton Pachal and Harold Phillipoff. Instead of looking for retribution, Armstrong threatened to bench any player who wanted to fight. "So he took the fear out of us," Boudreau said. "And we just skated and won 7-3."

It was easy to follow the coach. This was Armstrong, the legendary captain of the Maple Leafs and a four-time Stanley Cup champion. He was the man who told Boudreau he was a good captain, the man who protected him from hecklers in the stands at a game in Oshawa.

He was also the man Boudreau tripped over during a practice before the OMJHL playoffs, falling on one of his skates and suffering a long cut below his right eye. It left Boudreau with double vision for the next month. But there was no way he was going to miss that Memorial Cup and be in position to set a record that all his kids now know about. It's a mark he hopes won't be broken.

Five goals. And amazingly, a minus-1 rating. "That goes to show you my whole career, what it was like," Boudreau said. "It was a precursor."

BY ERIC STEPHENS

> "IN THE QUEBEC LEAGUE THEY SCORED A LOT, SO YOU LOOKED AT THEIR NUMBERS. 'OH, THESE GUYS ARE REALLY GOOD.' AND THEN WE KICKED THEIR ASS."

DOMINIK HASEK

DOMINIK HASEK

FEBRUARY 20, 1998

 ## CZECH REPUBLIC 2 VS. CANADA 1

•••

There are a plenty of games throughout Hasek's Hall of Fame career that could easily be considered his best. For him, however, it's the one that brought pride – and eventually a gold medal – to his country.

"For me, it was even more special because I was 33, and I hadn't played for the Czech national team since 1990. I thought it was my last chance ever to win an Olympic medal."
—Dominik Hasek

It evolved into a superstition. Every night before a game at the 1998 Winter Olympics, Dominik Hasek would test his chess skills against Czech teammate Martin Rucinsky. As the ritual and the tournament wore on, it felt to them like they had to play on the chessboard if they wanted to win on the ice.

Hasek doesn't want to overanalyze, though. He won't say whether or not the concentration required in the board game aided his concentration on the ice. But as good as he said his record was against Rucinsky – 6-1 overall, not including ties – his performance was even better in net. There, Hasek went 5-1, with a 0.97 goals-against average and a .961 save percentage. That included a spectacular 2-1 shootout victory over the heavily favored Canada when he backstopped the underdog Czech Republic to a gold medal.

The stage couldn't have been bigger for Hasek or his hockey-proud country, politically free of Soviet influence for less than a decade and uncoupled from Slovakia just five years earlier. It was the first time NHL players were allowed to

compete in the Olympics, and that made the Nagano Games the most accurate test yet of each nation's talent on ice.

Hasek had been focused on the Olympics for months, in part to help him get through a rough patch in Buffalo. He had displeased many Sabres fans the previous spring by saying he wouldn't mind if popular coach Ted Nolan was gone the following season. So when Hasek began the 1997-98 season with a subpar 6-10-3 record, a 3.12 GAA and an .898 SP, he heard plenty of boos on home ice.

By December, however, Hasek had found his game. He silenced critics with six shutouts that month, and just prior to Nagano he went eight games without a loss. Studying the roster of every national team, though, Hasek was a realist. "Of course I was dreaming about gold, but I thought any medal would've been fantastic," he said. "One thing is a dream, the other is what I thought would be success."

After a solid round-robin, the Czechs looked like anything but medallists after the first period of their quarterfinals against the U.S. "When the Czech people talk about this game, they say it was the worst first period we ever had," Hasek said. "We were terrible."

The dressing room was quiet after the period, until captain Vladimir Ruzicka broke the silence with a simple message. "He said, 'C'mon boys, let's play hockey. What are you doing? Do what we can do. Get on the ice and just play hockey,' " Hasek explained. "It was something we wanted to hear. We came back on the ice, and after that we were the best team in the Olympics."

The Czechs stormed back for a 4-1 win, setting up the memorable semifinal showdown with Canada. "Against USA, it was up and down, crazy hockey," Hasek said. "Against Canada, it was a more strategic game. Nobody wanted to make any mistakes. There were some chances but not many."

Hasek blanked the Canadians for nearly 59 minutes, and it looked as if an early third-period goal by Jiri Slegr might be enough to eliminate the tournament favorite. But with goalie Patrick Roy on the bench, Eric Lindros threw the puck into the slot from behind the goal line and Trevor Linden's wrist shot deflected into the net off a Czech defenseman's stick with just over a minute to go. "It was a lucky goal because it hit my friend Richard Smehlik – I don't remember playing more games with anybody other than Richard Smehlik," Hasek said of his teammate in Buffalo as well as in international competition. "It hit his stick and ended up in the top shelf on my left side corner."

A 10-minute overtime settled nothing. Then came the shootout.

Hasek learned which shooter he would be facing only as each jumped over the boards, none of whom turned out to be Wayne Gretzky. Coach Marc Crawford's decision not to tap The Great One for the shootout has been second-guessed since, but it didn't matter to Hasek at the time. He wasn't focused on whether he'd be facing the NHL's all-time scoring leader. "I didn't pay attention to whether Wayne was going to shoot,"

Hasek said. "It didn't come into my mind. Nothing."

The NHL had yet to embrace the shootout to settle tie games, so it wasn't as if Hasek had a complete book on what to expect as Theo Fleury, Ray Bourque, Joe Nieuwendyk, Lindros and Brendan Shanahan each skated toward him in turn. "With Theo Fleury, I made a good save with my shoulder," he said. "He tried to put it above me, and I just kept my shoulder up."

Czech forward Robert Reichel then scored what would be the only goal of the shootout, and Bourque, hoping to change that, skated toward Hasek to start the second round. "I sort of expected him to shoot somewhat high because I know he could hit whatever he wants from the All-Star Game skills competition," Hasek said. "So I got my arms very high, and he hit a little bit on my left arm."

After Hasek played Nieuwendyk's backhand move perfectly, forcing him to shoot wide, Lindros came within an inch of beating him when his shot clanked off the iron. Even the goalie isn't sure if he got a piece of the puck before that. "He was coming so quickly so I tried to cover my five-hole and he surprised me," Hasek said. "Maybe I made a save. I made my last-resort move, where I throw my body and my catching glove, but to be honest, I think he was skating so fast he had no time to put it up high and he hit the side of the post."

Jagr then hit the post, setting up the final shooter for Canada. "I know Brendan Shanahan had good hands, so I just tried to move outside and get his speed and be sure I covered my five-hole," Hasek said. "He made his move to the forehand, and I was there. I was ready."

Checkmate.

It would still take a 1-0 victory over Russia before the Czech Republic earned the gold medal, but Hasek sees the shootout win over Canada as his greatest game. Not because of his performance – "I think I had many games similar to this

> "FORTUNATELY, THE PILOTS HAD CASH WITH THEM, OR WE WOULD NEVER HAVE GOTTEN BACK TO CZECH REPUBLIC."

one," he said – but because Canada was the tournament favorite, and the victory meant so much to his country.

Hasek saw firsthand what the impact was back home. When the Czechs reached the final, president Vaclav Havel dispatched a plane to Tokyo to bring the players to Prague if they won gold. The jet ended up having to make a refuelling stop in the middle of Russia, and the journey almost ended there. "Fortunately, the pilots had cash with them," Hasek said, "or we would never have gotten back to Czech Republic."

In Prague, players had a private audience with Havel and a public celebration that filled Old Town Square with 140,000 fans. The next night, there was also a small reception in Hasek's driveway back in suburban Buffalo after his long journey home. "There were Czech flags on the houses, on the garage doors, and there were people, 10 to 15 kids and neighbors waiting for me," said Hasek, who spent about 10 minutes with the welcoming committee. "It was nice, but at the time I was so tired I said to my son, 'I just need to go sleep.' "

BY DAVID POLLAK

RED BERENSON

NOVEMBER 7, 1968

 ## ST. LOUIS 8 VS. PHILADELPHIA 0

•••

On a bumpy road trip where nothing was going right, Berenson changed
the momentum by tripling his goal output at that point in the season.
And he did it in a single night.

*"I felt good proving something, but then I realized, 'Geez, I'm not going to be able
to do this every night.' I finished in the top seven or eight in scoring, I believe, that year.
I think I had 35 goals, but that one game was the game that got me started."*
—Red Berenson

Every time Red Berenson took to the ice, hoping to spark a strong comeback for the Blues, there they were: Ed Van Impe and Joe Watson, the Philadelphia Flyers' premier defensemen. Berenson couldn't escape the matchup.

It was the latest obstacle in an up-and-down start to the season for the St. Louis Blues. They'd played their first road game of the month in Detroit, but despite a feel-good hat trick performance from Camille Henry, they only tied the Red Wings. Three days later, they left Pittsburgh with a 3-1 win over the Penguins but capped off the night in a Philadelphia hotel that was suffering from a power outage. "It was a trip where everything wasn't necessarily working out right," Berenson said of the long and winding journey. And it was reflective of their season thus far.

Through the 1968-69 season's first 11 games, Berenson had managed only three goals, but his main concern wasn't necessarily to personally elevate his play on Nov. 7 against the Flyers – a team that St. Louis had a budding rivalry against.

More importantly, he wanted to jumpstart his Blues. So when he finally solved the Van Impe–Watson duo late in the first by scooting around Van Impe and beating Flyers goalie Doug Favell with a backhanded shot, Berenson thought, "Thank God, I can still score."

Berenson became the only NHLer to score six goals in a road game, boosting the Blues to an 8-0 triumph that night on Broad Street. He was only one goal shy of the NHL record set by Joe Malone in 1920 and came oh, so close to tying the feat as one of his shots connected with the crossbar late in the game.

As for most of the others? They went in off of line rushes, 3-on-2 advantages and a breakaway. All came at even-strength – there were no power play markers, zero tap-ins and not a single empty-netter. It turned out that Berenson had reignited not only his team but also himself.

Berenson enjoyed a four-goal outburst in the second period, and after the Blues filed off the ice for the final intermission, defenseman Doug Harvey playfully told him, "You know, this would be a good game if you weren't playing in it."

Laughter echoed around the dressing room. It was the type of camaraderie that existed among the players: good-natured ribbing that accompanied a we-before-me attitude under young coach Scotty Bowman.

Actually, Berenson's teammates seemed more excited about the offensive surge than the goal scorer himself. He exuded a workmanlike approach on the ice, reinforced by a disciplined routine off it.

Before every game, his meal was steak and salad with a baked potato. He walked around the city for an hour and then napped for another hour or two. But Berenson couldn't explain why some games felt different from others despite the consistency of his preparation. When he found a rhythm, however, it was as if he could do no wrong, as evidenced by goal No. 6.

A crack had sprouted in the blade of Berenson's wooden stick in the third, so he decided to call on his spare. It felt foreign, like the fit was designed for another set of hands on a different player. But the trusty center used it anyway. And as he motored down the boards in the closing minutes of the game, he aimed glove-side. He scored – just not where he intended. The shot sailed over the netminder's stick. "That's the way it goes when the puck is going in," Berenson said.

With even the home crowd cheering him on by this point – support he had never received as a visitor before – Berenson was given the green light by Bowman to hop over the boards late in the game to pursue a seventh tally. Ever the team player, though, he declined – he didn't want to spoil St. Louis goalie Jacques Plante's shutout bid.

BY SARAH MCLELLAN

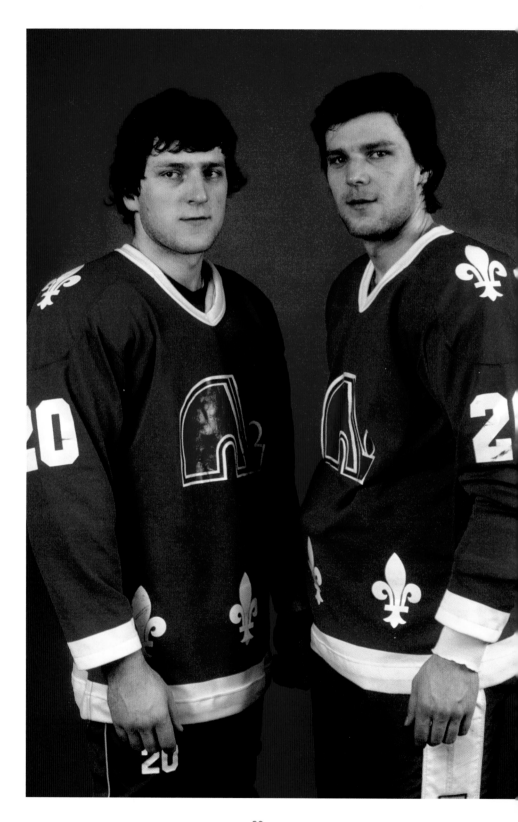

PETER & ANTON STASTNY

QUEBEC 11 VS. WASHINGTON 7

•••

Teams were seeing double in 1980-81. The Stastny brothers took the league by storm, combining for 194 points in their rookie seasons. Their most impressive feat? Torching Washington for 16 points just three days after lighting up Vancouver for 11.

"I had a six-point game and a seven-point game but not eight and certainly not six and then eight in consecutive games. To do it together with my brother pleases me even more. We won, and my brother and I had big games. The NHL made us the co-players of the week, and we were told it was the first time the league had honored two players. It's really stuck in my memory, and it's fun to go back and recall those moments."
—Peter Stastny

By all accounts, the Washington Capitals should have been on high alert when they faced the Stastny brothers on Feb. 22, 1981. After all, in the Quebec Nordiques' previous game, a 9-3 victory against the Vancouver Canucks, Peter and Anton had each scored three goals, with Peter drawing three assists and Anton two helpers. It was an 11-point night for the two first-year Nordiques players, who had defected from Czechoslovakia the summer before.

In what remains the most remarkable back-to-back performances for a set of brothers in NHL history, Peter and Anton each recorded eight points (seven goals, nine assists total) in an 11-7 victory over the Capitals two nights later, giving them a total of 27 points in the two games. Their 16 points against Washington surpassed the 13 points by the Bentley brothers (Max and Doug) set in 1942-43, and Peter's 14 points in those games remains an NHL record for a single player in consecutive contests. "To have two games

where you get 14 points with a hat trick in each game, and doing it with your brother, it was crazy," Peter said. "Today's game is so defensive. To have a game with that many goals would be a dream game today."

In 1981, teams averaged almost four goals per game apiece. By 2015-16, that number had slipped below three.

The Stastny brothers' route to Quebec is the stuff of spy movies. It wasn't purely the opportunity to play in the NHL that was responsible for their defection from Czechoslovakia in the summer of 1980. Their move was politically motivated. "It was complex," Peter said. "Basically, I was going for freedom and opportunity, but mostly freedom – not for myself, but mostly for my family. My wife was pregnant, and I was old enough to understand how evil the communist regime was and that I had no future in Czechoslovakia. I'm the type of person who is straightforward and value-based. People like me were a danger to society, to the regime. They were like ISIS: You were with them or against them – there was no in between. You had to have the same values as the regime did, which were atheistic. I was Catholic. I basically knew I had no future there and I wanted to provide a future for my family."

There had been interest in Peter from the NHL ever since he played for Czechoslovakia at the 1976 Canada Cup, but he didn't want to leave his home country. "I really had no choice," he said. "They threatened my career. They threatened that I would never play for the national team. Today, kids dream to play in the NHL and win the Stanley Cup. Over there, it was all about playing for the national team and going to the World Championship and the Olympics. That was the highest dream you had as you were growing up."

After threats were made against his family, Peter decided it was time to leave. In late August 1980, Peter and Anton, who were 23 and 21 at the time, accompanied their Czech club team, Czechoslovak Slovan Bratislava, to the European Cup final in Innsbruck, Austria. They had no plans to return home. Following an 11-1 loss to CSKA Moscow, the brothers attended a team dinner and then, instead of going back to the hotel, hooked up with Quebec Nordiques president Marcel Aubut and Gilles Leger, director of player development.

Early in the tournament, Peter and Anton had placed a call to the Nordiques saying they were prepared to defect and play for Quebec. Aubut and Leger hopped on a plane and were in Austria 24 hours later. "At that time, you have to remember the Russians and Czechoslovakian players couldn't come out, so it had to be hush-hush to get them," Leger said. "When you went over there, you had to be a little bit incognito. We were fortunate that we were able to get the three of them (older brother Marian joined the Nordiques in 1981-82) eventually to play as a line. It probably was the greatest brother line that ever played in the National Hockey League."

Peter wasn't afraid to defect, but he will never forget the fear he felt when he and Anton were temporarily separated following the loss to CSKA Moscow. "I lost my brother for about an hour, and I was scared," he said. "We were supposed to meet at midnight after the last game, and we decided to go a different route. We lost each other and it was crazy. It was like something out of a spy movie. There was military in Austria with machine guns."

"Sometimes it even comes back in my dreams, still," Anton said. "It wasn't necessarily scary, but a very, very challenging night – or should I say night and day, since we didn't sleep at all for 48 hours?"

The Stastnys were welcomed by Nordiques fans and became instant NHL stars. Playing on a line with Jacques Richard, Peter led the team in scoring his first season with 39 goals and 109 points in 77 games, while Anton was third with 39 goals and 85 points.

The reception they received from players around the NHL wasn't so warm, though. "The hockey wasn't easy, but I expected even worse," Peter said. "I was ready to protect myself on the ice. I never asked for any protection. I just wanted to play and to score goals and help my team win as many games as possible."

It soon became evident to all that the Stastnys wouldn't shy away from the rough going, and they were able to show their skill. "They were actually the first young Europeans that came over that were in the prime of their game," Leger said. "Peter and Anton were just getting acclimatized to the NHL, but they put on quite a show for a couple evenings, showing people they could play."

They sure could.

The Nordiques got off to a horrible 1-9-4 start, but by February they were starting to look like a potential playoff team. Quebec was at the end of a gruelling eight-game road trip and coming off back-to-back wins against the Colorado Rockies and Los Angeles Kings when they travelled to

> "WE WON BOTH GAMES, AND THE WINS WERE THE MOST IMPORTANT THING. BUT WE WERE LAUGHING. WHATEVER WE TOUCHED WENT IN THE NET."

Vancouver to face the Canucks. "We were in the race for the playoff spot," Anton said. "In a few months in the NHL, we quickly understood that playoffs and the Stanley Cup was what it was all about, so we had to play our best."

Peter scored three goals and added three assists, while Anton had three goals and two assists in the Nordiques' 9-3 victory. Then it was on to Washington. "We came from Europe where my longest trip was three and a half hours by bus, a couple of hundred miles at the most," Peter said. "That's what you do: You play one game and then you come home. Here, you've got these road trips where you play multiple games. They would tell us about all the travel in the NHL, and it was like fearmongering. But it was based on the truth."

The game against Washington was a wild affair. The Nordiques held a 2-1 lead after the first period and a 7-4 cushion after 40 minutes. They added three more in the third before the Capitals battled back with three of their own. An empty-net goal by Peter finished the goal-fest. "We skated well, despite playing the last game of a punishing West Coast–East Coast trip," Anton said. "The puck was following us, and we had a high shooting percentage, obviously."

The Stastnys' eight points each is an NHL rookie record that still stands today. "We won both games, and the wins were the most important thing," Peter said. "But we were laughing. Whatever we touched went in the net."

The following season older brother Marian joined the Nordiques, and the trio played as a line. "Looking at the three players, I always said Peter was the Mercedes, Anton was the Porsche and Marian was the Hummer," Leger said. "Marian did a lot of forechecking and was a pretty rugged player. Peter was a real worker and setup man, and Anton was a free spirit who would come in and score the goals."

Peter went on to win the Calder Trophy as the NHL's top rookie in 1981. It was the start of what would become a Hall of Fame career. He had 450 goals and 1,239 points in 977 NHL games and was inducted into the Hall of Fame in 1998. Anton, meanwhile, forged a pretty impressive NHL career, with 252 goals and 636 points in 650 games.

Peter now divides his time between Slovakia and the United States, where his children and grandchildren live. He has no regrets about leaving Czechoslovakia in 1980. "When they threatened me, I decided immediately and took off," he said. "It was by far the hardest but the best decision I ever made in my life."

BY MIKE BROPHY

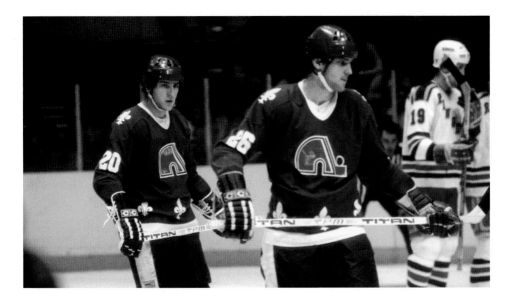

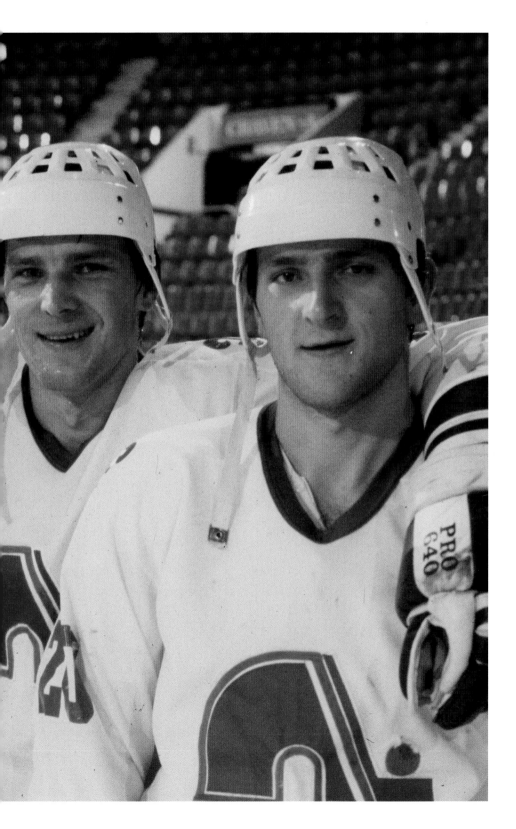

SHANNON SZABADOS

DECEMBER 26, 2015

COLUMBUS 3 VS. HUNTSVILLE 0

• • •

If play-by-play announcers didn't know how to pronounce her name before, they sure do now, because Szabados' 33-save shutout is in the record books – most notably the *men's* record books.

"I guess I had some idea that no one had a shutout, but it never really crossed my mind. To me, it was just another game until my phone started blowing up afterward and for the next two or three weeks, so that's probably what I'll remember most."
—Shannon Szabados

I deally, Shannon Szabados would have spent the holiday season with her family in Edmonton. But with the 2015-16 Southern Professional League schedule pausing for only two days over Christmas, the 29-year-old was forced to spend her time off miles away from home in Columbus, Ga.

Szabados and her Cottonmouths teammates celebrated Christmas with a party at coach Jerome Bechard's house and even hit the ice for practice on Christmas ahead of their Boxing Day meeting with the Huntsville Havoc. A regular workweek in spite of the holidays allowed the goaltender to stay in her routine leading up to her 12th game of the season, something she appreciated as a creature-of-habit netminder.

On the day of her third encounter of the season with the Havoc, though, she had an unplanned meeting. Szabados ran into Huntsville's play-by-play voice, A.J. McCloud, prior to puck drop and cleared the air about something that had been bothering her. "He always thinks I'm a guy," Szabados said. "If I watch the game tape back or my dad will write me and be like, 'Yeah, he still

thinks you're a guy.' The game before, I watched the tape, and he's like, 'Oh, Szabados makes a save, and he plays it to his defenseman!' Before the game, he came up to me, and he was like, 'Oh! Are you Shannon?' and I was like, 'Yeah! I'm a girl!' I had a chat with him, and he was also butchering my last name – I don't even know how he was saying it – so he asked me how to pronounce it."

Huntsville had a ticket deal for the Saturday night game, offering four tickets for $40 and as a result, the Havoc, who averaged about 4,000 fans a night at Propst Arena, had a sellout crowd of 6,256 in attendance to witness history. A full rink had Szabados, who had played in front of large crowds at both the 2010 and 2014 Olympics with Canada, excited for the occasion. "I like playing in big games and with lots of pressure," she said. "The more fans and the louder it is, the more focused I get. That night they were loud."

Szabados would need to be focused, as Columbus was outshot 27-15 through the first two periods. Ben O'Quinn got the Cottonmouths on the board in the second period, and they held a one-goal lead until Louis Belisle and Chris Rial scored third-period insurance goals. Szabados took care of the rest, turning aside six Havoc shots in the final frame. "I was trying to keep the guys in it. I think we had a pretty good third period," Szabados said. "We ended the game on the power play, which is nice to kind of solidify it."

Szabados' performance cemented her place in history as she became the first woman to record a shutout in a men's professional hockey league game. But she didn't fully grasp the significance of her win until she checked her phone after the game and saw a message from her dad: "Congratulations on the win, and the shutout – you just made history!"

And the messages continued to pour in, including ones from Hall of Fame goaltender Grant Fuhr, ex-NHLer Rob Schremp and analysts from around the hockey world, magnifying the importance of her accomplishment. "It was pretty overwhelming," Szabados said. "I saw it all over my newsfeed. My social media was blowing up. It was pretty cool. That was probably the best part of it, just seeing the impact that it had."

BY DHIREN MAHIBAN

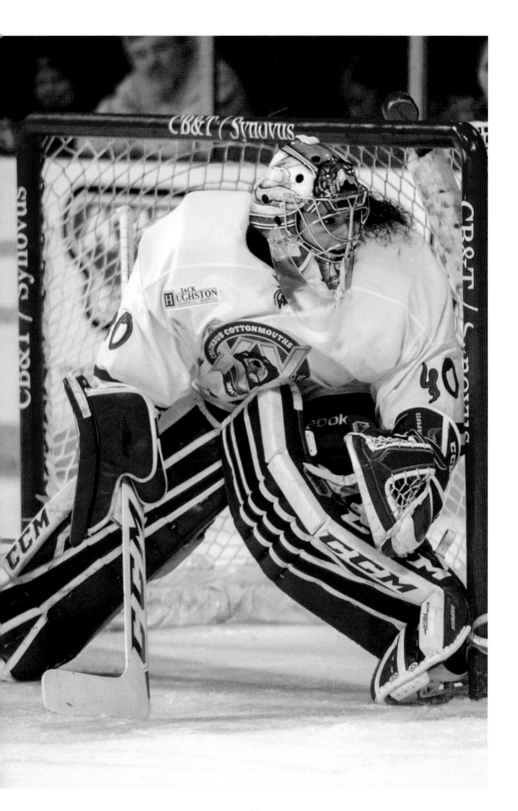

PATRIK SUNDSTROM

APRIL 22, 1988

NEW JERSEY 10 VS. WASHINGTON 4

•••

When Sundstrom leapt into the post-season record books – move over, Gretzky! –
it was a figurative twin killing. Not only did he set the record for points
in a playoff game, his eight in Game 3 of the Devils' second-round series came
with his twin brother on the opposing bench.

"Mario Lemieux, Wayne Gretzky and me – that's pretty good company.
When I scored the eight points in that game, I remember thinking that it wasn't such
a big deal, because I had seven in a game with Vancouver a few years earlier.
But looking back at it now, it's a pretty neat feat."
—Patrik Sundstrom

Usually, they would call each other at least a few times every week, not just to chat about hockey but to catch up on life. In April 1988, however, the phones at the homes of Patrik and Peter Sundstrom stopped ringing for the length of the brothers' seven-game playoff series. This particular matchup between the New Jersey Devils and Washington Capitals marked the first time in league history that twin brothers had faced each other in the playoffs. More importantly, though, it featured a game in which Patrik erased one of Wayne Gretzky's most impressive NHL records.

Ironically, there hadn't been a single fight in the seven meetings between the Devils and the Capitals during the regular season. Instead, the Patrick Division rivals saved their mutual hatred for what would turn out to be the most penalty-filled playoff series in the history of the NHL when they met in the second round. The seven-game series ended with 654 penalty minutes, the majority of which were taken by the Devils, who set a record for most PIMs in a single series by one team with 349.

The violence culminated in Game 3 at Brendan Byrne Arena in East Rutherford, N.J. The Friday night fight-fest lasted three hours and 25 minutes and featured 62 penalties and 231 penalty minutes. "Guys were genuinely trying to hurt each other out there, and things got out of hand pretty quickly," said Devils center Anders Carlsson. "We both had very tough teams, but the difference was that Washington's tough guys were also their best players. So when Scott Stevens, Dale Hunter and those guys were ejected from that game, we had a pretty easy path to victory. And Patrik was obviously the one who benefitted most from that."

Patrik did indeed. In between the fights, skirmishes and assaults, he piled up points like he was collecting stamps. After setting up linemate Mark Johnson for his fourth goal, the arena announcer told the New Jersey faithful that the 26-year-old pivot had just tied Wayne Gretzky for most points in a playoff game. And with two goals and five assists already to his credit in the third period, Patrik still had time to surpass The Great One. "Guys were chirping me on the bench, yelling that I had to get one more point," Patrik said, laughing. "We had already killed the game, so I think they were worried I was going to let down and save energy for the next game. They made sure I didn't."

With 5:46 left in the game, Sundstrom broke in from the right side and shovelled a backhand between goalie Clint Malarchuk's pads. The crowd went nuts and teammates cheered along. "Being a Swede, I was unaware of the record before they announced it," Patrik said of the record, which was equalled by Mario Lemieux the following year. "There was a lot of commotion in the arena afterward, and the guys were really happy for me, but we were in the middle of a tight playoff series, so I really had to put it behind me fast. It wasn't until after the season that it really sunk in – that I realized what I had accomplished. Today, I'm really proud of it."

And then there was Peter, Patrik's twin brother, sitting on the opposite end of the lopsided score. He shook his head in disbelief as he watched his brother torment the Capitals all night long. "It was ridiculous," Peter said. "Every time he stepped on the ice, they seemed to score. Early in the game, I was mad about it, but when the game was out of hand I actually started to root for him. I was happy when they announced he broke the record, but I obviously couldn't sit on the bench and smile about it. I smiled internally instead."

Today, Patrik is somewhat forgotten in Sweden for what he did during his NHL career. Although he accumulated 588 points in 679 NHL games with the Canucks and Devils, he's seldom mentioned among the great players of his generation, probably because he had his peak at a time when the NHL wasn't well covered in his native country. "People back home never realized how good he was, or how respected he was in the league. He was one of the best two-way forwards you could find in the game in those days," Carlsson said. "I'm incredibly happy he managed to get that record, so he could add something special to his legacy. Eight points in one playoff game – that's a record no one is ever going to beat."

BY UFFE BODIN

SERGEI FEDOROV

DECEMBER 26, 1996

 ## DETROIT 5 VS. WASHINGTON 4

•••

Plenty of players have had five-goal games throughout NHL history, but most were in blowouts. On this night, however, the Red Wings needed every one of Fedorov's five goals, including his overtime winner, to eke out a win.

"It was just an unusual night. All of a sudden, I scored two goals, and then I was in a mood to score more goals. The puck was going in for me. I think all my shots went in."
—Sergei Fedorov

When Sergei Fedorov does the math, it all adds up so symmetrically. Five goals, five Russians. 'The Russian Five.'

Hockey had become a paint-by-numbers game by the mid-1990s. With rapid expansion diluting the skill pool, coaches turned to smothering defensive styles as their system of choice, all but squeezing the offense out of the game. "Destroy hockey," was how Detroit Red Wings centerman Igor Larionov described the strategy.

In an effort to combat the uninspired frontlines of the game, Detroit coach Scotty Bowman came up with the idea of inserting the creativity of five Picassos into this scenario, and the result was truly a work of art. Bowman compiled a unit of five players from the former Soviet Union and then sent them over the boards and into the nightmares of opposing coaches. "It was like having five Gretzkys on the ice," said former Wings defenseman Paul Coffey.

This was a sentiment even the man himself wasn't about to debate. "They were better than any five-man unit I've ever seen in the NHL," said Gretzky.

And what a five they were. There were the legends, Larionov and defenseman Viacheslav 'Slava' Fetisov, whose battles extended off the ice as they fought the Soviet regime to gain the right to play in the NHL. There was 'The Vladinator', defenseman Vladimir Konstantinov, who gave no quarter and asked none. And there was the other 'Slava,' the mercurial Vyacheslav Kozlov, who flew under the radar but fired home so many big goals.

But the man who made it all go, the straw that stirred the drink, the piece that completed the puzzle, was Fedorov. He was "the total package for a player," according to former Detroit goalie Chris Osgood. "He was an unbelievable athlete, almost a freak of nature, really."

Fedorov's belated holiday gift to Red Wings fans was one that no other NHLer before or since has ever duplicated in a regular season game. On Dec. 26, 1996, Fedorov scored every one of his team's goals, including the overtime winner, in Detroit's 5-4 win over the Washington Capitals.

Of the 44 players who've scored five goals in an NHL game, Fedorov is only the second to score every single one of his team's goals, after Maurice

Richard. He was the finisher and The Russian Five his catalysts. Working together, they earned 13 points. "We played for each other, we skated for each other – and the team," Fedorov said.

These Wizards of Oz were masters of confusion who practiced patience and never took low-percentage shots. Finesse was their trademark, as per the Russian style of training and play. Hockey to them was a form of jazz as they scatted about the ice, creating on the go and improvising with the puck.

They were five of a kind, you might say, and Fedorov was the ace in their hand. Lots of players can skate with blinding speed. Many others can deliver the high-end skill required to finish a play. But Fedorov was among the rare few capable of delivering both at the same time.

Scoring all five of Detroit's goals when the team needed every one of them is now a memory that warms Fedorov's heart. "This whole night, it was very exciting," Fedorov recalled. "When you score in overtime, it's always a big celebration, because that means it's time to close the office and send everybody home happy."

The true testament to his skill was the fact that less than a year earlier, Fedorov had come within one failed penalty shot attempt of doing exactly the same thing. He'd scored all four goals in a 4-4 tie against Los Angeles on Feb. 12, 1995, a game in which he was foiled by Kings goalie Kelly Hrudey on an overtime penalty shot. "I remember that," Fedorov said. "There was big pressure, big focus on me and I didn't score. It was disappointing.

Fedorov's memory of this night was much more satisfying. "I was a happy kid," he recalled. "I was so excited. It was wonderful."

BY BOB DUFF

CHRIS TERRERI

MARCH 28, 1985

 ## PROVIDENCE 4 VS. BOSTON COLLEGE 3

• • •

Terreri almost singlehandedly carried his college team all the way
to the NCAA Div. I final. But he's better known for sparking a now longstanding
habit among goalies along the way.

*"You know what, it's weird. People have told me that I was the first goalie
to place a water bottle on the top of the net, and I guess I just did it, but I never
realized that it wasn't done before."*
—Chris Terreri

When Chris Terreri arrived at the rink, he felt well rested and confident. It was the morning of the biggest game of his collegiate career, and the NCAA schedule had given the teams nearly a week off between games, even during the single-elimination national championship tournament. Since there wasn't much of a pre-game skate in college hockey, the morning consisted of laid-back meetings and casual preparation for the game. It felt typical, even routine to the 20-year-old all-American goaltender. Yet after setting an NCAA record and starting a trend that found its way all the way up into the NHL's goaltending ranks, Terreri's performance that day would become the stuff of college hockey lore and urban legend.

Leading up to the game, Terreri's play with the Providence Friars had been anything but typical. Less than a week earlier, he'd made 50 saves to cap off a two-game quarterfinal series win over the Michigan State Spartans, the top-ranked team in the country at the time. A couple weeks earlier, he faced more than 50 shots in his Friars'

double overtime win over the Boston College Eagles for the Hockey East Championship.

Nothing about the game to come was typical, either. A berth in the final and a chance at the NCAA title was on the line. The Detroit Red Wings' Joe Louis Arena, which had opened six years earlier, was the theater. Boston College, owning a superior 28-15-2 record, was once again the opponent.

And Terreri wasn't the only confident one. He knew the Eagles would be assured that if they dominated play like they had in the Hockey East Championship that it'd work out their way. So if Providence were to advance to the final, the netminder's performance couldn't be typical, even by his standards.

The game, though blurred by more than 30 years, the entirety of an NHL career and two Stanley Cups as a backup to Martin Brodeur with the New Jersey Devils, lives on in Terreri's memory in its individual moments. Now the Devils' goalie coach, he looks back and remembers the big saves, the long overtimes, the goals and the water bottle legend. Jumping out to the early lead was paramount when goals were hard to come by. The Friars scored three goals in a 2:15 stretch to take a commanding 3-0 lead early: a quick backhand from leading scorer Tim Army, a floating shot from center ice from defenseman Peter Taglianetti and a rebound goal from Rene Boudreault.

Once again, however, the Eagles controlled the play and the shots piled up. But Terreri felt like he was getting into a rhythm. He was seeing the puck, and he felt good as his workload increased, but he knew it was a double-edged sword. "I'm certainly not the biggest goalie in the world, especially back then," said Terreri, all of 5-foot-9. "It starts to wear you down."

Late in the first period, Boston College's leading scorer Scott Harlow beat Terreri to cut into the Friars' lead. In the second period, the shots kept coming, but Terreri was up to the challenge. In the third, the Eagles dictated the territorial game and the zone collapsed. Then Boston College freshman Dan Shea scored twice, both off the rush to tie the game at 3-3 to force overtime.

Before overtime even began, Terreri had another 50-save game under his belt. His Providence team had been outshot 53-15 at the end of regulation. The ice, it appeared, truly was tilted. "They might have been the best team we played all year," Terreri said. "They had a tremendous hockey team."

> "THEY MIGHT HAVE BEEN THE BEST TEAM WE PLAYED ALL YEAR. THEY HAD A TREMENDOUS HOCKEY TEAM."

In the moment, Terreri hadn't realized how great he'd been. He'd given up three goals, the game was tied and there was still hockey to be played. Through two overtimes, Terreri had made a dozen more stops. As the saves piled up, Terreri rested his water bottle on top of his net to stay hydrated more easily. He was the first goalie to do so, and it caught on quickly, with NHL goalies adopting the practice in the 1985 playoffs.

Finally, in the third overtime, just 33 seconds in, the onslaught was over. It was a simple play but one the Friars had been unable to make outside a three-minute stretch in the first period. Army made a pass to defenseman Paul Cavallini, who sent a shot in from the left-wing boards. In front, right winger Artie Yeomelakis picked up the rebound and tucked the puck around Eagles' goaltender Scott Gordon.

For the second time in a month, Providence had upset Boston College. Only this time, the Friars were headed to the National Championship. Terreri finished with 62 saves – a Frozen Four record that stands more than three decades later – on his way to being named the tournament's MVP.

BY SCOTT WHEELER

ÉRIC DESJARDINS

JUNE 3, 1993

MONTREAL 3 VS. LOS ANGELES 2

•••

The Habs' 1993 Stanley Cup run was jam-packed with headlines:
Patrick Roy's heroics, the team's 10 straight overtime wins and the illegal
stick call on Marty McSorley. Lost in it all has been Desjardins' record-setting
night in Game 2 that changed the course of the final.

*"It's something you want to do – you want to prove yourself every game, prove that you
belong in the league, prove that you're elite. That game proved I had my spot."*
—Éric Desjardins

É ric Desjardins had never been booed until Game 3 of the 1993 Stanley Cup final. When the series shifted to Los Angeles, the Kings faithful, experiencing a Cup final for the first time, made note of the player who almost singlehandedly won Game 2 back in Montreal and greeted him with a chorus of boos that rattled the then-23-year-old defenseman.

Maybe he should have seen it coming.

In Game 2, Desjardins played one of the single best Stanley Cup final games ever. He scored all of the Canadiens' goals in a come-from-behind 3-2 overtime win that evened their series with the Kings 1-1. It was the first time a defenseman had scored a hat trick in the final, and it hasn't been done again since. It also helped turn the series in Montreal's favor. Instead of heading back to L.A. down 2-0, the series was tied and the Habs won the next three games to win their 24th Stanley Cup.

Despite his great game – and the implications it had for the series – Desjardins wasn't prepared to be greeted with boos at the Great Western Forum. "I was shocked," he said. "They were booing me because of that game. It was another thing

I had to get over. It took me a few shifts to say 'OK, you have to play now. You won't score three goals every game. Just get back to your game and play the way you played the whole season.'"

The unfriendly greeting in the City of Angels was another surprise in a whirlwind few days for Desjardins. While his Game 2 heroics have become the stuff of legend in Montreal, it didn't dawn on Desjardins right away what he had done. He said it all happened so fast that he didn't realize he had accomplished a historic feat.

His first goal came late in the first period and gave Montreal a 1-0 lead. The Kings took a 2-1 lead midway through the third and things were looking dire for the Canadiens. Then the Canadiens dug into their bag of tricks. The entire team knew going to L.A. down 2-0 would be disastrous, and they were looking for something – or someone – to spark the team. They got both.

Late in the third, reportedly on the advice of Montreal captain Guy Carbonneau, coach Jacques Demers called for a measurement of the curve on Kings defenseman Marty McSorley's stick. It was a risky call. The rules at the time stated that if the stick was illegal, McSorley would be penalized, but if it was legal, the Canadiens would receive a two-minute bench minor. While Carbonneau and Demers get most of the credit for the gutsy decision, Desjardins said it was made as a team, as a "last resort." In a dramatic scene, McSorley's stick was deemed illegal, sending the Canadiens to the power play with 1:45 to go. Just 32 seconds later, with the net empty and Montreal on a 6-on-4 advantage, a Desjardins one-timer from the point found its way through a crowd and past Kings goalie Kelly Hrudey to tie the game.

Overtime didn't last long. Just 51 seconds in, Desjardins took a pass from Benoit Brunet, skated in and beat Hrudey five-hole to win the game. "I scored my first goal, and there was a lot of hockey left to play," Desjardins said. "Then the next two goals happened so quickly I never really thought about it until it was all over. I remember after the overtime everyone was on the ice. We were all together. I remember Vincent Damphousse realizing I had the three goals and saying, 'You're sick, you're sick.' He was all pumped, we were all excited."

Since it all happened so fast, the night isn't something Desjardins has thought about much. It certainly started out as any other game. Desjardins was in his fifth NHL season, and despite still being a relative youngster, he was wise enough to give up on pre-game superstitions and routines. Earlier in his career, he thought they had become a distraction. If he played poorly, it was easy to blame his performance on something he did or didn't do leading up to the game. He gave all that up in time for the 1992-93 season, and had been having a career year up until that point. His 13 goals and 45 points led all Canadiens defensemen, and he wouldn't eclipse those single-season totals until later in his career with the high-flying Flyers of the late 1990s.

The Habs' 1993 playoff run is also largely remembered for the Canadiens' NHL-record 10 overtime wins. Although Desjardins wasn't feeling particularly special or prepared for Game 2 in the Stanley Cup final, he did feel that something special was happening for the team. That feeling, though, began in the opening round. After falling behind 2-0 to the Quebec Nordiques, the Canadiens won Game 3 – in overtime, of course – and started believing right then and there that they could go on a long playoff run. Desjardins remembers Demers instilling confidence in the team, no matter how often they fell behind or how many times they needed to be rescued in overtime.

Unlike other record-setting single-game performances, Desjardins' feat will very likely one day be equalled or eclipsed. Prior to his hat trick, seven other defensemen had scored three goals in a playoff game (Brian Leetch became the ninth in 1995), but none had ever done it in the final. For now, Desjardins is quite content to have his name in the record books.

Twenty-three years later, he still has yet to sit down and watch his most memorable game in full. Living in Quebec, he sees plenty of highlights of the goals, especially the overtime winner, when it's playoff season. Watching it is not on his immediate to-do list, though. "I'm not old enough yet – I'm still in my 50s," he said. "I still remember bits. But one day, I'll probably watch that game and some of the other games in that series."

One thing he remembers for sure is how that single game made him feel like he belonged in the NHL. He'd played in the All-Star Game the season before, but that game for the ages – in the Stanley Cup final, no less – was what made him truly feel like he had a spot among the elite in the NHL.

Desjardins played only one more full season with the Canadiens before being sent to the Flyers in a blockbuster deal that brought Mark Recchi to Montreal. It was with Philadelphia that Desjardins had arguably his best years. He was a two-time second-team all-star and consistently

> **"I WAS SHOCKED. THEY WERE BOOING ME BECAUSE OF THAT GAME. IT WAS ANOTHER THING I HAD TO GET OVER."**

among the league's best defensemen. He went to the final again in 1997, but the Flyers were swept by the Detroit Red Wings. He had other great nights over his 17-year career, but nothing like that night in June 1993. He also never had another hat trick in his career. "Not even close," he said.

BY IAN DENOMME

MILT SCHMIDT

B ### BOSTON 8 VS. MONTREAL 1

• • •

They sure don't make them like they used to. The term "gentleman" is an understatement when describing guys like Schmidt, who risked a Hall of Fame career to serve his country.

"It just goes to show you that once the game is over, it's finished and we're good friends."
—*Milt Schmidt*

The game itself wasn't terribly memorable for anything that happened on the ice. It was between a league power and a doormat. For one of the few times in NHL history, the Montreal Canadiens were looking up at almost all the rest of the league in the standings, and the Boston Bruins were enjoying life as a perennial contender. The New York Americans, who would fold after the season to create the Original Six, were the only team doing worse than Montreal.

Even the result of the game that night of Feb. 10, 1942 in Boston was predictable. Going in, the Bruins had dominated the Canadiens with five wins and a tie and had outscored them by a 23-10 margin. The Habs were in the midst of the fourth-worst season in their 100-plus-year franchise history and had earlier in the season been beaten 10-0 by the Detroit Red Wings and 9-2 by Chicago. In 1941-42, they started 1-10-1 and established what still stands as a franchise mark for futility: beginning a season with a 0-4-1 record at home. Maurice Richard was still a year away from playing for the team, and if there are any dark days in the history of the franchise, the 1930s and early 1940s certainly qualify.

The Bruins, meanwhile, were the defending Stanley Cup champions. Bill Cowley, who would hold the league's all-time points record for quite some time, had won both the scoring championship and the Hart Trophy the season prior, and Frank Brimsek was in the midst of winning his second Vezina Trophy. Even with Cowley, leading scorer Roy Conacher and Hall of Fame defenseman Dit Clapper out of the lineup with injuries, the 20-11-5 Bruins were primed to slaughter the 10-22-2 Canadiens, which they did by a score of 8-1.

That game might have gone down in history as just another one of the more than 52,000 games that have been played since the NHL began in 1917-18. It would have been that way if not for one of those magical moments after the game that had never happened before and will almost certainly never be duplicated. It was a moment so heartwarming, so spontaneous, that people still talk about it almost 80 years later. It was a moment that Milt Schmidt, with his voice fading and his body 98 years on Earth, speaks of as though it happened last night. "It was one of the best nights of my life," Schmidt said. "The Montreal Canadiens taking us on their shoulders and carrying us off the ice – what more can you ask for? I'll never forget the Canadiens for that as long as I live."

So here's the backstory. Both Schmidt and childhood friend Woody Dumart were pressed into service with Canada's military for the Second World War and they were being joined by their linemate and friend Bobby Bauer. They had earned the rather politically incorrect nickname of 'The Kraut Line' in Boston, but the three of them had been thick as thieves even earlier, going back to their baseball days together in Kitchener. "Bobby was the manager of the Waterloo Siskins baseball team, and I thought it would be nice to play baseball for him," Schmidt said. "Woody was a softball player, and he could really hit the ball. He was a lefthander. I was a pitcher, and I got along pretty well myself."

The three of them knew that night would be the last game of the season for them. What they didn't know was whether or not it would be the last NHL game they ever played together. They were due to ship out the next day but asked for some time off and were given a month to spend with their families prior to going to war. All told, The Kraut Line ended up with 22 points that night, with Schmidt assisting on a second period goal by Dumart and a third-period goal by Bauer. He also assisted on Jack Shewchuk's goal in the second. Dumart finished the night with a goal and three assists, while Bauer had two goals and two assists.

Then, after the game ended, the three were presented with their paycheques for the rest of the season, plus a bonus. And with no warning, the Canadiens players gathered around the three men and spontaneously started putting them on their shoulders to carry them off the ice. The Bruins players joined them, and the crowd at Boston Garden roared its approval. Schmidt was just 24 and in the prime of his career. He had already won two Stanley Cups, he was nearly a

point-a-game player in a league where scoring was at a premium, and he was on a team that was primed to contend for years to come. Bauer was a week away from turning 27, and Dumart had just turned 25 a couple months before. All were in the prime of their careers, only to be called away to serve their country.

The three exchanged their uniforms for army fatigues and would be joined a little more than a year later by Brimsek, who was a member of the U.S. Coast Guard and found himself in the South Pacific. Schmidt said none of them ever thought of the possible perils they faced or the careers they were leaving behind. Schmidt said that if others in Canada were being called to duty, there was no reason why they shouldn't have been. "The person who was most upset about it was my mother," Schmidt said. "I came to Kitchener and she asked me, 'Why are you home so early? Are you going somewhere?' And I said, 'Yeah, Ma, I'm being posted overseas.' When I was waiting for the car to pick me up, I asked her, 'You know, Schmidt sounds pretty German. Is it OK with you if I change my name to Smith?' She said, 'Change it to whatever you want.' But as I was leaving, I thought to myself, 'If this name is good enough for my father and my mother and brothers and sisters, it's good enough for me, too.' "

It wasn't long before Schmidt found himself stationed at a place called Middleton-St. George in northern England, a bomber command station that had been the target of bombings. You know those posters that are all the rage now that say "Keep Calm and Carry On"? Well, that was actually a campaign launched by the British government during the war to inspire people like those of Middleton-St. George.

Schmidt and his teammates returned home three years later. Schmidt married Marie Peterson, who had waited back home for him. "She was lovely," he said. He carried on his NHL

> "THE MONTREAL CANADIENS TAKING US ON THEIR SHOULDERS AND CARRYING US OFF THE ICE – WHAT MORE CAN YOU ASK FOR? I'LL NEVER FORGET THE CANADIENS FOR THAT AS LONG AS I LIVE."

career, and although he never won another Stanley Cup, Schmidt twice put up 60-point seasons and won the Hart Trophy in 1950-51.

There were tense moments as his ship approached harbor with him and 1,500 soldiers on board, but for the most part Schmidt and his station remained safe. The Hall of Famer mostly played sports, including cricket, in northern England, and worked to keep things safe in that part of the world. "We were never bombed, but they fired on us a couple times," Schmidt said. "We got really good at hiding under the bed."

BY KEN CAMPBELL

MARC-ANDRÉ FLEURY

JUNE 12, 2009

PITTSBURGH 2 VS. DETROIT 1

●●●

Ever the jokester, Fleury took time to play a prank on some unsuspecting hotel guests ahead of the biggest game of his career – the one in which he made his most memorable save to win the Stanley Cup.

"That's why we play. When you're a kid, you dream about playing in the NHL, but you want to win the Cup. You play on the street, and you play to win the Cup. Then when you do it for real, it's amazing."
—Marc-André Fleury

A bucket of water. A prankish payback. Odd things for Marc-André Fleury to be thinking about in the hours before he started in goal for Game 7 of the Stanley Cup final, a game he helped the Pittsburgh Penguins win 2-1 against the Red Wings and would for years be recognized as his most memorable game. But that's what went down the afternoon of June 12, 2009 in a Detroit hotel.

It started off like any game day: with a morning skate at Joe Louis Arena. "I just tried to treat it like a regular game," Fleury said. "Go to the rink, practise, lunch with the guys – same routine."

The annoying twist came when he returned to his hotel room. His afternoon nap, a staple among NHL players, wasn't going to happen right away. "There were so many people in for the game," Fleury said. "I remember it was loud in the hallway. I was a little stressed out. I like to sleep. I finally fell asleep."

When he woke, Fleury was ready to face Detroit in the winner-take-all game. First, though, he had a mission. "Those people making

noise at the hotel, before I left, I filled a bucket of water and put it up against their door," Fleury said. "I knocked and ran away so when they opened the door a big bucket of water fell in their room."

Imagine that. On the way to such an important, career-shaping game.

In some ways, that was Fleury keeping things routine. Although serious about his craft as a goaltender, he has a loosey-goosey side to him and is one of his team's known pranksters.

With the hotel incident satisfyingly put to rest, Fleury turned his focus to the game. Pittsburgh was a young team led by budding superstar centers Sidney Crosby and Evgeni Malkin. Fleury was their 24-year-old franchise goalie, and he entered the game under a lot of scrutiny.

There were questions about whether he could win such a big game, and questions about whether he could win against the seasoned Red Wings stars at Joe Louis Arena. Fleury had a career 3.64 goals-against average and .887 save percentage at 'The Joe,' and playoff games in Detroit hadn't been kind to him.

Fleury and the Penguins had lost in the final against the Red Wings a year earlier. In Game 1 of that series in Detroit, Fleury tripped as he led the team out of the dressing room, falling flat onto the ice. He gave up four goals that night in a loss.

Before Game 2, he comically made an exaggerated effort to step carefully and safely onto the ice. Pittsburgh lost again. His only win in Detroit that series came in triple overtime in Game 5.

In the 2009 rematch, Fleury again took losses in Games 1 and 2 at Joe Louis. In Game 5, he gave up five goals on 21 shots and got pulled during a 5-0 loss. Pittsburgh won its three home games, setting up the decisive Game 7. Once Fleury got to Joe Louis late that afternoon, any lingering demons in the old barn were left at the door. "Everything before that didn't matter," Fleury said. "It was just that one game. We only had to win one there. That's what mattered."

A scoreless first period only raised the intensity. The breakthrough opening goal didn't come from Crosby or Malkin. Nor did it come from Detroit's Henrik Zetterberg, Pavel Datsyuk or Nicklas Lidstrom – a defenseman with a laser shot who gave Fleury his biggest test in the final seconds.

It was hardworking Penguins winger Max Talbot who made it 1-0 less than two minutes into the second period. Talbot, a fellow French-Canadian, also happened to be one of Fleury's best buddies. "You always wonder which way it's going to go and who's going to get the first one," Fleury said. "I was real happy that we scored, but to see Max do it... he always gave all he got."

Talbot secured his spot in Cup final lore when he scored again midway through the second period. Detroit's Jonathan Ericsson cut the deficit to 2-1 with 6:07 left in regulation. "The heart gets going a little bit," Fleury said. "There wasn't that much time left. I was looking at the clock. 'Just hold on for a little bit and then they'll pull the goalie, so it will be 6-on-5. Just got to hold it off for six minutes.'"

Adding to the drama, Crosby spent the third period planted at one end of the visitor's bench after a knee injury knocked him out of the game. How cool and collected was Fleury? "I was so in the game, I didn't even notice that much," he said. "I just thought, 'Hmm, I haven't seen Sid in a while.'"

The Red Wings did, of course, pull goalie Chris Osgood. The game came down to a faceoff to Fleury's left with 6.5 seconds remaining, that one-goal Pittsburgh lead staring down from the scoreboard. Zetterberg beat Penguins center Jordan Staal, and the Red Wings' Brian Rafalski let loose a slapshot from the right point.

The rebound floated toward the left circle – and Lidstrom. Fleury was near the far post, seemingly giving Lidstrom a gaping target. "I had time to think a little bit," Fleury said, alluding to the feeling elite athletes sometimes have that time is moving slower. "I gave up the rebound, and I remember seeing him. I saw he was a lefty. I thought about just sliding in a split (to get his right pad down along the goal line), but I thought that he was probably going to shoot high because he has time."

Fleury opted for a full-body lunge to his right that put him in position to stop the shot that, indeed, Lidstrom lifted just as time was expiring. It was Fleury's 23rd and biggest save of the night. "It might not have been my best game – the most shots, the most saves – but just to win was incredible," Fleury said.

During the days of celebration that followed, Fleury carried a reminder of Lidstrom's shot. "I got it in the ribs," Fleury said. "I had a bruise after the game. I still had the mark on my ribs for a couple of weeks. It was a good souvenir."

BY SHELLY ANDERSON

"I KNOCKED AND RAN AWAY SO WHEN THEY OPENED THE DOOR A BIG BUCKET OF WATER FELL IN THEIR ROOM."

PAVEL BURE

RUSSIA 7 VS. FINLAND 4

•••

Revenge is a dish best served cold, and Bure dished out an ice-cold entrée of five goals at the 1998 Olympics. After being shut out by Finland 4-0 in the 1994 bronze medal game, Russia found itself in a semifinal rematch, where 'The Russian Rocket' stole the show.

"Nowadays, Vladimir Putin rewards our athletes with bonuses and new cars,
but in those days we were just happy to be playing for our country. The happiest days
of my life were when my children were born. But that day in Nagano is something
I will remember for the rest of my life."
—Pavel Bure

A Calder Trophy race cost him an Olympic gold medal in 1992. A drive to the Stanley Cup final was the focus of his attention when the 1994 Olympics rolled around. And in an exhibition game against the United States prior to the 1996 World Cup of Hockey, he suffered a kidney contusion and was unable to play in the tournament.

That made wearing the letter C for Russia at the 1998 Olympics extra special for Pavel Bure, who was 26 at the time. Alexei Yashin had been the favorite, and Bure's nomination had come as a bit of a surprise. "It was such a big honor to be named the captain of the team," Bure said. "I had been watching hockey since I was six years old. I'd seen guys like Boris Mikhailov and Slava Fetisov, and I tried to learn something from them."

Injuries and the refusal of several of its stars to participate as a result of a dispute with the Soviet Ice Hockey Federation left Russia with a second-rate lineup. So drastic were the cuts that an all-star team could have been formed from the missing, which included goaltender Nikolai Khabibulin, defensemen Slava Fetisov, Sergei Zubov, Vladimir Malakhov and Oleg Tverdovsky, and forwards Alexander Mogilny, Alexei Kovalev, Igor Larionov and Slava Kozlov.

Russia had failed to win a medal of any color at the Lillehammer Games in 1994, losing 4-0 to Finland in the bronze medal game, and its players were eager for revenge when the two countries met in the 1998 semifinal in Nagano, Japan.

This time the explosive Bure and his team had the Finns on their heels from the opening whistle and the game turned into his personal shootout as he dazzled a crowd of over 9,000 fans, mostly Japanese.

He gave Russia a 1-0 lead early in the first period, putting home a rebound on a power play. After taking a perfect pass at center ice from Dmitri Mironov, Bure then turned a brilliant pivot into a breakaway, and in less than four seconds Finnish goalie Jarmo Myllys was digging the puck out of the back of the net. That made it 2-0. Capitalizing on a mistake by Kimmo Timonen, Bure completed a hat trick, streaking in alone to put the puck between Myllys' pads at the 59-second mark of the second period. "It was extra special because it was the first Olympics in which NHL players were allowed to play," Bure said. "So all of the best players in the world were there."

Finland, however, boasted a superb NHL line with players Teemu Selanne, Saku Koivu and Jere Lehtinen and was able to come back and tie the score twice.

Russia finally went ahead for good on a goal by Andrei Kovalenko, but Bure took off like a jet again and went solo to beat Myllys off a Teppo Numminen turnover. "I was always trying to get open for a breakaway," he said. "When I got it, I was going so fast I didn't even think about whether I was going to go forehand or backhand."

With just five seconds left on the clock, 'The Russian Rocket' fired his fifth goal of the game into an empty net from his own blueline. The final score was 7-4.

Russia ultimately fell 1-0 to the Czech Republic in the gold medal game, but with nine goals in the tournament Bure was a shoo-in when votes for the best forward were counted.

A Russian player hadn't come close to Bure's effort in one Olympic game in 42 years prior, and to this day his performance hasn't been matched. Vsevolod Bobrov once scored four goals in a 10-3 romp over Switzerland at the 1956 Games in Cortina d'Ampezzo, Italy, the first in which the Soviets competed, but that was as close as anyone has come. The nation had won seven hockey golds and nine straight medals in nine Olympic Games from 1956 through 1988 as a powerhouse, but none with the revenge-driven dazzle of Bure.

Incredibly, when the International Ice Hockey Federation released its list of top 100 moments in international hockey history in 2008, Bure's amazing performance was not included. Even more incredibly, however, is that while it was clearly his greatest professional game, Bure's five goals don't represent his personal best. "I remember a game when I was 12 years old playing for the championship of Moscow against a team called Lokomotiv, and I managed to scored nine," he said. "We won 30-0."

BY DENIS GIBBONS

BILL MOSIENKO

MARCH 23, 1952

CHICAGO 7 VS. NEW YORK 6

•••

Toward the end of the season, Mosienko had been thinking about how to leave his mark on the game. And, boy, did he ever find a way – all it took was 21 seconds to etch his name into hockey history forever.

"I was thumbing through the record book, and I remarked how nice it would be to have my name in there with some of the hockey greats. But I just figured it would never happen – and then it did, 48 hours later."
—Bill Mosienko

It was March 23, 1952, and Bill Mosienko was restless. As he pondered the final game of the regular season against the Rangers after another miserable campaign for his Chicago Black Hawks, he reflected on a decent career that was lacking a legacy.

The sad sack Hawks had qualified for the playoffs only four times in Mosienko's 14 seasons, and there seemed to be no hope for a Stanley Cup in Chicago anytime soon. Now, at age 30, when players around him began contemplating retirement, the 5-foot-8 160-pound right winger felt unfulfilled.

Mosienko would rather not be remembered for breaking his leg in the 1947 All-Star Game or for winning the Lady Byng Trophy in 1945. As a member of the famed 'Pony Line' with the Bentley brothers (Max and Doug), he achieved scoring success but won no championship trophy to complement it. He was awarded a gold watch once, but that was for winning a speed skating contest against fellow NHL players.

But there was one more game to play, and 'Mosie' knew that he had the Rangers' number.

And Chuck Rayner wasn't playing goal for the fifth-place Rangers. Instead, 20-year-old rookie Lorne Anderson from the Atlantic City Sea Gulls of the Eastern League was starting his third NHL game. Unfortunately for him, it was his last.

Nicknamed the 'Blonde Blizzard,' Mosienko prepared mentally and physically, even if it was a meaningless end-of-year contest. An estimated 3,254 fans showed up to see the two doormats of the league go through the motions – or so they thought. Referee Georges Gravel officiated a penalty-free game that saw the Hawks come back from a 6-2 deficit to squeak out a 7-6 win. More astoundingly, however, Mosienko set an NHL record that likely will never be broken.

After assisting on Gus Bodnar's goal 44 seconds into the game, the mediocre Hawks allowed the surprisingly high-flying Rangers to score six of the next seven goals. Mosienko, sensing that his pre-game talk had been a futile gesture, scored at 6:09 of the third period then again at 6:20 and yet again at 6:30, all assisted by

Bodnar. Ranger defenseman Hy Buller, playing on a bad ankle, was a turnstile each time Mosienko flew by him for a goal.

In 21 seconds, Mosienko had shattered the record for fastest three goals by a single player. The previous individual mark was set by Red Wing Carl Liscombe in 1938 in 64 seconds.

Mosienko described his stunning feat in an interview with *The Hockey News* a couple weeks later. "The first of the three was the climax of a planned play," he said. "Gus passed to me. I beat the New York defenseman and wrapped it in. On the next faceoff, Gus got the puck, I wheeled, broke for the blueline, took the pass and shot. Then on the third, the faceoff went to George Gee on the left wing, he went over the blue line, I made my move and he laid a perfect pass on my stick."

On the next faceoff, Bodnar passed again to the confident Mosienko, who wristed a shot off the post. Mosienko wanted that one badly, which would have tied his career best of 32 goals, set in his rookie season. It would've been four goals in 28 seconds and would've tied the game as well.

Hawks coach Ebbie Goodfellow then replaced the line, kidding Mosienko about hitting the iron on the last shot: "What the heck happened, you in a slump?"

After the first goal, Mosienko retrieved the puck. It was only his 29th goal, and he had no real reason to keep it, but perhaps he had a premonition. The second goal signified his second 30-goal season, so Mosienko picked up that puck, too.

Following the third goal, teammate Jimmy Peters yelled from the bench, "Mosie, Mosie! Grab that puck! It's a record!"

Mosienko later held the three pucks in one hand, with his lucky stick in the other, and posed for a photo to capture the moment for posterity. "It was something to dream about," he said.

BY PAUL PATSKOU

JIMMY PETERS YELLED FROM THE BENCH, "MOSIE, MOSIE! GRAB THAT PUCK! IT'S A RECORD!"

SAM GAGNER

FEBRUARY 2, 2012

EDMONTON 8 vs. CHICAGO 4

•••

Down early against the powerhouse Blackhawks, Oilers coach Tom Renney shuffled his lines and stuck Gagner between two unfamiliar wingers. Gagner's following two periods of work would warrant a text message from Wayne Gretzky.

"It's something I still look back fondly on. It gives me confidence today. When a game like that happens, you want to keep it going. And when things don't go as planned, you look back at games like this one and gain confidence."
—Sam Gagner

Beer wasn't allowed in the Edmonton Oilers' dressing room. Or maybe it was. The rule on alcohol in the backstage had changed enough times during Sam Gagner's tenure with the Oilers that he might have been breaking it when he cracked open a can of suds in the late hours of Feb. 2, 2012. But no one was going to tell him otherwise – certainly not Joey Moss, the team's dressing room attendant, who joined Gagner for a brew long after his teammates had left. Rules or no rules, an exception had to be made. It was time for the two friends to relax and soak in what had just transpired. It isn't every day that a player scores eight points in a single game.

In fact, no one had accomplished that since Mario Lemieux did so in April 1989, a good three months before Gagner was even born. But setting records and making history were the furthest things from Gagner's mind when he lit up the Chicago Blackhawks with four goals and four assists.

Considering the season he was having, it was just the boost the young center needed. Gagner missed the end of 2010-11 with a severed tendon and was sidelined to start 2011-12 with a high ankle sprain. With Ryan Nugent-Hopkins hurt, Gagner was put on a line with Taylor Hall and Jordan Eberle. It was the best game of Gagner's life, and he only needed two periods to accomplish it. "I wasn't too happy after the first period," he said. "I hadn't played very well. Our team had a sluggish start. That's when Tom Renney switched lines up going into the second, putting Taylor, Jordan and I together. We had a lot of chemistry and were able to bury our chances."

The Blackhawks, a team two years removed from winning the Stanley Cup and perhaps still sore about losing the previous two games to the Oilers – including a 9-2 drubbing in October – held a 1-0 lead after the first period. Just 40 seconds into the second, Chicago scored again. Then Gagner took over, netting a goal and assisting on two others. Not ones to give it up easily, the Blackhawks tied it going into the third, a challenge to which Gagner attributes some of his success that night. "It helped that it was a pretty tight game from start to finish," he said. "It was always in reach for Chicago, and that's what forced me to put my foot on the gas."

Gagner never slowed, exploding for another three goals and two assists in the third period. Even after his hat trick goal, Gagner told his teammates that he wasn't done. "It was just one of those feelings," he said. "I was really confident that night. When you have a game like that, you just want to keep pushing yourself."

In the end, Edmonton won the game 8-4, with Gagner involved in every goal by his team. He received a standing ovation from the crowd and was named the first, second and third stars of the game. Perhaps an even bigger accolade was receiving congratulations from both Paul Coffey and Wayne Gretzky, who shared the team's rec-

ord for most points in a game with eight. Coffey phoned Gagner the next day, and The Great One sent a text saying, "Congratulations. Enjoy the moment. Keep it going."

Gagner, indeed, kept it going. He had a pair of goals and an assist two nights later against the Detroit Red Wings. His three points that game made it 11 straight Oilers goals in which he had a point, a new franchise record. "It's one of the greatest feelings," Gagner said about his eight-point game. "When you have that many people cheering for you, it's a special feeling... It's a memory I will never forget."

BY SAL BARRY

JIMMY WAITE

JANUARY 1, 1988

CANADA 3 VS. SOVIET UNION 2

•••

A year after Canada and the U.S.S.R. engaged in one of the ugliest brawls hockey has ever seen, Waite stood tall for the Canadians as the rivals clashed again on New Year's Day, this time in Moscow, in what became a world juniors instant classic.

"Getting disqualified and getting redemption the next year in their homeland –
the whole story made it so special. I think that's why it's regarded as one
of the biggest gold medals in history."
— Jimmy Waite

On New Year's Day, 1988, while strapping on his pads and pulling his Team Canada sweater over his goaltending equipment, 18-year-old Jimmy Waite was thinking of only one word: discipline.

Outside of the Ron Hextalls and Billy Smiths of the hockey world, discipline, or a lack thereof, isn't often associated with goaltending. For Waite, however, the meaning of the word rang loud and clear, because it was the absence of discipline – not his own but a whole team's – that had nearly cost him and his Canadian teammates their shot at making an entire nation proud. Almost one year earlier to the day, on Jan. 4, 1987, Waite had watched as his first chance at World Junior Championship gold disappeared in a flurry of fisticuffs that would become infamously known as the "Punch-Up in Piestany."

During that unforgettable brawl, Waite stood at the blue line, concerned that getting involved in the fracas would get him tossed from the game. His hope was that he could still lead Canada to gold, but he wouldn't get his chance. Instead, the lights went out, the game was called and every-

thing Waite and his teammates had worked for was wiped from the history books. Canada and the U.S.S.R. were disqualified and their statistics stricken from the record. The implications of the brawl threatened to reach past 1987, too. "I remember after that tournament hearing that we were all going to be disqualified for the next year," Waite recalled.

The International Ice Hockey Federation eventually backed off from banning Canada and the U.S.S.R. from the 1988 event, in part because Moscow was to play host. The initial 18 months of suspension were reduced to six, and Waite, who had avoided suspension anyway on account of his not dropping his gloves, was set to try for gold again the following year.

At the time, the world juniors were decided in a round-robin tournament. There were no elimination games, and medal winners found the podium thanks to their play over several contests. Still, Waite and the Canadians knew no match mattered as much as the Jan. 1 meeting with the Soviets on their rival's home turf. As the tournament approached, both teams understood the

New Year's Day game would almost assuredly decide who won gold. "Being in Russia, in Moscow, after that brawl against the Russians – that made that game even more special for us," Waite said. "We wanted to beat those guys so badly, and I'm sure they wanted to beat us, too."

Canada went into the competition, especially their battle with the U.S.S.R., with revenge on their minds. They knew full well it had to come up on the scoreboard, too. The nerves were ever-present for the Canadians, all of whom were several thousand kilometers away from home, staying in a palatial hotel neighboring Moscow's Red Square and tasked with making up for the previous year's blunder. "We felt like we let the country down in that big brawl," Waite said. "To redeem ourselves is why we were so thankful to get a second chance at it."

The Soviets were clear favorites in the tournament. They were a team built for destruction. Led by two of the greatest Russian-born players of all-time, Alexander Mogilny and Sergei Fedorov, the Soviets spent the entire tournament picking opponents apart. They convincingly defeated all comers, including a 6-2 drubbing of Finland, who played Canada to a draw. Until the tournament began, though, Waite and company had only a minor understanding of how talented the Soviets were, in large part because of the lack of media coverage of the tournament. "Thank God," Waite said. "We might have been more scared if we knew."

As powerful as the U.S.S.R. team was, though, the crowd made taking on the Soviets even more intimidating. The raucous group of supporters in Moscow made it clear how important the Jan. 1 game was and showed their distaste for the Canadians. Waite and his teammates were met with consistent, ear-piercing whistling throughout the game, a show of audible hatred from the fans that went unmatched in any other tournament game. The Canadian team, Waite included, was bent on not letting the fans or the Soviet players get in their heads.

> "BEING IN RUSSIA, IN MOSCOW, AFTER THAT BRAWL AGAINST THE RUSSIANS – THAT MADE THAT GAME EVEN MORE SPECIAL FOR US."

By the time the puck dropped, Waite couldn't hear a thing. He was focused on the task at hand. So set was he on righting 1987's wrong that he began to believe nothing could get by him. "You always wish to be able to get those kind of games, in that zone," Waite said. "When it happens, it's a great feeling."

Even with the Russians as favorites, Canada stormed out to a 2-0 lead on the strength of goals by Trevor Linden and Theo Fleury, who Waite said stood out as the most outstanding players on the big ice in Moscow. But the Russians, with their incredible firepower, refused to go quietly. Waite was beaten twice in the second period, and the pressure of the moment felt insurmountable.

The U.S.S.R. outshot Canada 17-4 in the second, and the puck appeared to have a magnetic attraction to the blades of the Soviet players while bouncing haplessly off the sticks of their Canadian counterparts. The nervousness was beginning to affect Canada, and the only relief was a Marc Laniel goal on one of Canada's four shots in the period.

The third frame was no different. Waite watched shot after shot fired his way by outstanding players such as Fedorov, Mogilny, Valeri Zelepukin and Dmitri Khristich. And then the save happened.

The Soviets were buzzing around in the Canadian zone when the puck was rocketed on goal from the right blue line. The shot missed wide, but Waite had committed. Down near his left post, he made a move toward the pipe, thinking he could seal off the quick shot he was sure was coming. Waite watched in horror as the Soviet player scooped the puck and instead swung around the goal. A pass spilled out in front and all Waite could do was dive and pray. "I was able to squeeze in my arm at the last second to deflect the puck out into the corner," he said.

Of all the saves he made, it's that save which Waite remembers most, and it was one of 38 he made to help Canada to a 3-2 victory over the

U.S.S.R. Canada soundly defeated Poland and West Germany en route to gold, and Waite was named the tournament's best goaltender. After the disappointment of 1987, the weight of their accomplishment wouldn't hit Waite until he arrived back on Canadian soil. "Nothing else can beat that moment," he said. "Coming back and seeing all your family and friends, all of the whole country is really behind you. You don't realize how big it is until you get back home."

BY JARED CLINTON

KRIS RUSSELL

MARCH 5, 2015

CALGARY 4 vs. BOSTON 3

•••

Stepping in front of hundreds of shots is usually something asked
only of goalies, but Russell has faced his fair share, too.
He knows how to take one – or 15 – for the team.

*"It's probably the only game I'll have a record from, which is cool. After you're done, it's
special to have that record and be recognized that way, but blocking shots – to have 15 a
night – obviously the game's not in your favor, and you're not playing the way you want."*
—Kris Russell

Most hockey pools are basic: Goals, assists and points are the key components. Some integrate other elements, such as penalty minutes, plus-minus and game-winning goals. Kris Russell's friends have made sure to add one very specific factor to their pool: blocked shots. "I think it's so I'm relevant in the draft," joked Russell, who set an NHL record by blocking 283 shots during the 2014-15 season with the Calgary Flames.

Whenever Russell racks up a slew of blocks in a game, text messages of thanks are common, but his performance against the Boston Bruins late in the 2014-15 campaign was worth more than just a note.

When the Flames came away with a 4-3 shoot-out win in Beantown, David Schlemko's highlight-reel winner in the eighth round, coming in his Flames debut, was the huge talking point. It was just the third game for the team without captain Mark Giordano (lost for the season due to a torn bicep muscle), and that win continued the rebuilding club's unexpected run to the Stanley Cup playoffs.

But one number jumped off the scoresheet: 15. That was how many shots Russell had blocked – an NHL record. As a team, Calgary's skaters blocked 37 shots, eight of them by Russell's defense partner Dennis Wideman. By comparison, Flames goalie Karri Ramo stopped 34.

Russell is the first to admit he'd rather be firing pucks on net than risking a broken bone, but there's something to be proud of when putting oneself in the line of fire. "Look at puck-possession teams like Chicago," Russell said. "I don't think Duncan Keith has ever seen 15 shots against him in a game, nevermind blocked that many. But you have to do everything you can to not get scored on."

Fortunately for Russell – who wears extra protection on his feet, inside his shin guards and on his wrists – that night didn't result in any issues. "Guys were asking how sore I was, and I was fine. All of them hit me in the right spot," Russell said. "A few games later, I had just one block. It got me on the wrong spot and I was limping around."

BY RANDY SPORTAK

HAYLEY WICKENHEISER

FEBRUARY 20, 2014

CANADA 3 VS. UNITED STATES 2

•••

With what would be the fourth straight Olympic gold medal hanging in the balance, Wickenheiser led the way as she and her teammates dug deep into the lessons they had learned on the brutal mountains of British Columbia.

"A lot of times in hockey, things don't go your way. You get a bad bounce, you get scoring chances and you can't score. And then there are games when everything goes your way. And that game – for the second half of that third period – everything went our way."
—Hayley Wickenheiser

Hayley Wickenheiser's shoddy mountain bike slipped and skidded as she rode through another stream of mud washing down the mountain trail. The rain was coming down heavy, and the wind was strong and hard in her face. Her Canadian women's hockey teammates were right there with her, struggling through the same miserable conditions. Some of them shouted words of encouragement, while others simply put their heads down and drove forward.

It was July 2013, and this was the last, toughest test of a gruelling 40-day Olympic boot camp – a 1,300-meter ascent up Apex Mountain, a Tour de France–ranked mountain biking trail in Penticton, B.C. Wickenheiser would later call it the worst hell she'd ever been through. But even as the merciless wind and rain slowed her progress, she knew there was no turning back. Team Canada was going to reach the top of the mountain.

The women were quiet as they returned to their dressing room and stripped off their shoulder pads for intermission. Brianne Jenner and Marie-Philip Poulin accepted a few taps on the shin pads for a job well done – so far. They'd scored two late goals for Canada to force overtime against the United States in the gold medal game of the 2014 Winter Olympics in Sochi, Russia.

Jenner potted her goal on a fluke bounce off U.S. defender Kacey Bellamy's shin pad with about three and a half minutes left to go in the third, cutting the Americans' lead to 2-1. That bit of luck sparked the Canadians to believe, as Wickenheiser put it, that they could "definitely come back" against their archrivals. "We weren't in unfamiliar territory when we were down a couple goals," Wickenheiser said. "When we got the first goal off a lucky bounce, that turned the tables."

Canada pulled its goalie for the extra attacker and nearly paid for it, when an American clearing attempt skittered down the ice and hit the post. But Canada kept the pressure on, and Wickenheiser's linemate, Poulin, finally tied it up with under a minute left.

As Wickenheiser entered the dressing room before overtime, she saw a quiet confidence in her teammates, a determination to finish the comeback they'd started. "Everybody knew what had to be done," she said.

The 20-year national veteran told her teammates to load up on carbs and sugar, so they'd be ready for a long overtime battle against the Americans.

Wickenheiser's longtime teammate Caroline Ouellette reminded everyone of the brutal climb up Apex Mountain they'd made together the summer before. The one where they made it right to the top. "This was our Apex Mountain," Wickenheiser said. "It was pouring rain, terrible conditions, and it just summarized all the training and all the tough stuff that we went through as a team."

A few players nodded. They all remembered. They knew their job wasn't finished. "We are not going back from here," Wickenheiser said. "We went through hell for too long to get to this point to lose."

Both sides traded chances and penalties during the 4-on-4 overtime. Canada was called for a cross-check about six minutes in, and then an American player went to the box seconds later on an even-up call. Canada coach Kevin Dineen leaned heavily on Wickenheiser's two-way skills during the ensuing 3-on-3, playing her at center with Meghan Aghosta on her wing and Laura Fortino on defense.

At the end of a long 3-on-3 shift, Wickenheiser pounced on a missed U.S. one-timer in the Canadian slot, and took off on a breakaway up the ice. U.S. forward Hillary Knight came driving after her, closing the gap as Wickenheiser carried the puck over center ice. "I had a million things going through my mind," Wickenheiser said. "'Win the Olympics.' I think that crossed my mind once or twice."

Wickenheiser had just crossed the blueline when Knight caught up. Knight's right foot clipped Wickenheiser's skate, throwing her off balance and dropping her to the ice. The referee called a penalty shot, then changed the call almost immediately to a cross-checking penalty.

Wickenheiser was back on the ice for the power play, leading the attack in the American zone. She dished the puck off to a teammate and set herself up as a screen in front, while Poulin, Rebecca Johnston and Fortino formed a passing triangle.

Canada worked the 4-on-3 perfectly – a flurry of quick passes in the slot would have been tough enough to track for goaltender Jessie Vetter without Wickenheiser standing a foot outside her crease. Poulin was deft and sure, snapping a quick shot into an open short side to cap off a perfect play and win the game 3-2. "It was a pretty surreal moment," Wickenheiser said. "The greatest comeback I've ever been a part of."

BY JOSH ELLIOTT

> "WE WEREN'T IN UNFAMILIAR TERRITORY WHEN WE WERE DOWN A COUPLE GOALS. WHEN WE GOT THE FIRST GOAL OFF A LUCKY BOUNCE, THAT TURNED THE TABLES."

RON TUGNUTT

MARCH 21, 1991

QUEBEC 3 vs. BOSTON 3

•••

He didn't win the game, and he lost 10 pounds in the process,
but Tugnutt proved that he belonged in the NHL with a 70-save performance,
even if he had to wait for his standing ovation.

*"With a funny last name like mine, people tend to laugh. And maybe more people
recognized the accomplishment because of the name. But for me, it was about making
a statement that I belonged in the league, that I was earning my stripes.
That's what made that day so special to me."*
—Ron Tugnutt

R on Tugnutt was anxious to get it over with. It was overtime, and the faceoff was to his left. Leaning on his pads in utter exhaustion, Tugnutt glanced toward center ice, then over at the faceoff dot to his left and back to center ice again as Bruins fans momentarily abandoned their seats, paying tribute to a legend.

The woeful Quebec Nordiques, destined to settle at the bottom of the NHL standings for a third straight year, were visiting Boston Garden, and Guy Lafleur, an icon on a league-wide farewell tour, was the recipient of the standing ovation.

Tugnutt, hunched over in the Nordiques' crease, just couldn't enjoy the moment. His physical, mental and emotional capacities were virtually spent, and there was the unfinished business of settling a game against the powerhouse Bruins. Leading up to the faceoff, a Ray Bourque shot from the point through a screen had somehow found Tugnutt's depleted 5-foot-11, 165-pound frame. It was a common sight on that Thursday night in early spring of 1991.

"Even pucks I wasn't seeing were hitting me," Tugnutt recalled. "I was like, 'Gee, I feel really good right now. They're not beating me.' "

Post-game, Tugnutt stepped on a scale and made a quick calculation in his head. Eight... nine... 10 – he had lost 10 pounds over the course of the 3-3 tie. The game felt as if it had lasted a lifetime, which is easy to understand given that he was facing sharpshooters Bourque and Cam Neely.

Prior to the game, Tugnutt had felt the pressure. Nerves were uncalmable on game day, especially at the Garden. In an effort to quell his anxiety, the goalie tried to adhere to his usual routine as much as possible.

Morton's was a staple of Tugnutt's Boston itinerary over the course of his 16-season career. The steakhouse, two miles from the arena, was always a comfortable retreat the night before a start.

Tugnutt shared a dressing room with backup Jacques Cloutier following his arrival at the rink, two hours prior to puck drop. The visitor's room at the Garden was notorious for being small – it had space to house every player, and yet not quite enough to squeeze in the goalies.

Still uneasy, Tugnutt set up shop at his stall. He grabbed a couple of sticks and began taping. Stretching followed. He tried not to think about how he was soon to be trapped in a near rectangle nine feet shorter and two feet narrower than the league's standardized rink size. It was a foreboding environment for an unproven 23-year-old.

Tugnutt was attacked at all angles by the Bruins, yet amassed an unbelievable 70 saves – a total that still stands as the most in NHL history by a goaltender for a non-losing effort in a regular season game. Boston's 73 shots fell 10 short of the NHL benchmark, coincidentally also held by the Bruins for their 83-shot barrage against Sam LoPresti of the Chicago Black Hawks way back in 1941.

A digital sign noting LoPresti's place in hockey lore caught Tugnutt's eye in the early stages of the five-minute overtime period, and suddenly everything felt so real. "I'm thinking, 'My God, this guy gave up only two goals and he had 80-something shots on him? I'm going to have to kick out some more rebounds if I want to get there.' "

> "I'M THINKING, 'MY GOD, THIS GUY GAVE UP ONLY TWO GOALS AND HE HAD 80-SOMETHING SHOTS ON HIM? I'M GOING TO HAVE TO KICK OUT SOME MORE REBOUNDS IF I WANT TO GET THERE.' "

Sixty-one shots in regulation and another nine in 4:50 of overtime paved the way for the Bruins' last-ditch charge. To cap off an NHL-record 19-shot effort, Bourque launched a one-timer from the hashmarks toward a screened Tugnutt. Overextending his catching arm, Tugnutt flashed leather to snag the airborne disc with eight seconds remaining. For the second time that night, Bruins fans stood up to applaud and show their appreciation for an opposing player.

Neely voiced his disbelief as the Nordiques' goalie glided away, flipping the puck in and out of his Hall of Fame-bound glove. Bourque shook his head in disbelief. "I always believed in myself," said Tugnutt, who added his last two saves after that charge, "but when you do something like that, you say, 'I do belong with these guys.' And that's a great feeling."

Finally, the anxiety had been swallowed up. He could savor the moment. And this time, the moment belonged to him.

BY JOHN MATISZ

FRANK MCGEE

JANUARY 16, 1905

OTTAWA 23 VS. DAWSON CITY 2

• • •

McGee led the charge in one of the biggest routs in hockey history, scoring 14 goals after the opposition questioned his greatness. Dawson City was lucky he only had one good eye.

"McGee put on a one-man show...that was brilliant in the extreme."
—Gordon Headley

H all of Fame executive Tommy Gorman never forgot the experience of seeing Frank McGee for the first time from the cheap seats in Dey's Arena in Ottawa. "McGee's appearance was dramatic," Gorman remembered in the *Ottawa Citizen's Weekend Magazine* on May 4, 1957. "His white pants had been pressed to a knife-like edge, his blond hair combed to perfection, his boots shined and his stick freshly taped. As he skated to join his team, from all parts of the arena came the famous Ottawa cry: 'McGee! McGee! What's the matter with Frank McGee!'"

The point of the cheer was that there was *nothing* the matter with McGee, even if he was blind in one eye from an earlier injury. (Gorman doubted the story, though it seems clear McGee was at least somewhat visually impaired.)

McGee played just four seasons at hockey's highest level, from 1902-03 through 1905-06, but his Ottawa Silver Seven won the Stanley Cup all four years. Seasons were short, and McGee played just 23 regular season games in total but added 22 more in the playoffs. Sources vary, yet he scored between 131 and 135 goals.

On Jan. 13, 1905, Ottawa faced Dawson City in the opener of a best-of-three Stanley Cup challenge. The Silver Seven won 9-2, but most accounts claim the game was closer than the score indicates. "McGee did not exert himself," noted the *Ottawa Journal.* He scored only once. According to legend, the Klondike players were unimpressed heading into the second game of the series on Jan. 16. "Word was whispered around that McGee was 'not so hot,' and that all those stories of the country's greatest center were a lot of rubbish," said sportswriter Gordon Headley in a retrospective for the *Journal* on Dec. 12, 1936. McGee was "incensed over these remarks," according to Headley, and took his anger out on the Klondikes.

It was 3-1 Ottawa when McGee scored the first of four goals that led the Silver Seven to a 9-2 lead at halftime. He added 10 more, including eight straight in a span of just over eight minutes, during the second half. Despite a final score of 23-2, no one left early. "Everybody stayed to the end," noted the *Journal* the following day, "for it was too good a chance to see the great line of (Alf) Smith, (Harry) Westwick, McGee and (Frank) White working so perfectly."

BY ERIC ZWEIG

MAURICE RICHARD

MARCH 23, 1944

MONTREAL 5 VS. TORONTO 1

• • •

A slow start to the first-round series had some Habs fans worried, but Richard quickly put those worries to rest with an all-star performance in Game 2. Literally. He was named all three stars in the game on his way to winning his first Stanley Cup.

"Whether this was the greatest game I ever played is for others to decide, but from my viewpoint it was because at the end of the game the three-star selection went as follows: third star: Richard; second star: Richard; and first star: Richard. Others said the final score was Rocket 5, Toronto 1. From a very personal point of view, it was my most memorable night, but from a team perspective, the real icing on the cake was beating Toronto and then Chicago to win my first Stanley Cup."
—Maurice Richard

Not long after Maurice Richard scored an astounding five playoff goals in his Montreal Canadiens' 5-1 victory over the Toronto Maple Leafs on March 23, 1944, someone suggested to Montreal public relations director Camille DesRoches that the kid had become some kind of god. "Richard is not God," DesRoches reverently shot back. Overhearing the conversation, Habs GM Frank Selke Sr. gave a cultural perspective: "No, Richard is not God," Selke quipped, "but in Quebec he is very close to the pope."

And just to underline the point, the irrepressible Rocket would go on to score 50 goals in 50 games during the following season. Yet when one considers what transpired in the French-Canadian's career just a few years earlier, it's hard to believe that Richard ever made it to the NHL at all. "Many people had said that I would never be an NHL star, and I couldn't blame them a bit," Richard told me when we worked together

on his autobiography, *The Flying Frenchmen.* "From my rookie season (1942-43), I suffered what seemed like an endless series of injuries."

The Montreal media was just as skeptical. One headline blared the bad news, "Richard Too Brittle for Pro Hockey." Fortunately, Richard had two pivotal people in his corner. GM Tommy Gorman and coach Dick Irvin realized that their gifted right winger had too much talent to be dismissed so soon. When his sophomore campaign began, Richard showed up healthy and motivated. Richard replaced Charlie Sands on a line with Elmer Lach at center and Toe Blake, Richard's longtime idol, at left wing on what later would be dubbed 'The Punch Line.' "Once the 1943-44 season started," Richard said, "I got hot and wound up with 32 goals in 46 games."

What's more, he got himself a moniker that would become better known than his real name. Although many versions of the story have emerged through the years, Richard said the nickname 'The Rocket' developed during a practice session. Irvin usually had The Punch Line skating against a trio comprising Phil Watson, Murph Chamberlain and Ray Getliffe. Time and again, Richard would dazzle them with his footwork until one of them cracked, "Watch out, here comes The Rocket!" A reporter picked up on the chant, and a deathless nickname was born.

Speed was only one of the young star's abilities. He became so strong that teammates joked that he had muscles in his hair. Writing in the *Montreal Gazette,* columnist Dink Carroll picked up on another asset. "Richard has a habit of going around a man on one foot and holding him off with one hand," Carroll wrote. "That trick requires strength of arm and strength of leg."

By playoffs time, the first-place Canadiens were pitted against their archrivals, the Leafs, which wasn't exactly good news for Richard. Among Toronto's best players was left winger Bob Davidson, regarded as one of the most efficient defensive forwards in NHL history. "He was also one of the finest and cleanest players I ever skated against," Rocket conceded. "He did his job against me well – hard but clean and never handed out a dirty check."

So adept was Davidson in the opener on March 21, 1944, at the Montreal Forum that the Leafs came away with a stunning 3-1 win. Richard was kept scoreless, and there was fear in Montreal that Toronto might make it two in a row when the clubs met again two nights later, especially after Davidson blanketed Richard in the scoreless first period of Game 2.

But early in the second frame, The Punch Line went to work, with Blake setting up Richard, who beat goalie Paul Bibeault with a deke and then a

> "MANY PEOPLE HAD SAID THAT I WOULD NEVER BE AN NHL STAR, AND I COULDN'T BLAME THEM A BIT."

shot at 1:48. Just 17 seconds later Lach and Blake fed each other until Rocket was spied. Bang! A quick pass and Richard had his second goal. Toronto got one back, but at 16:46 Blake and Lach prompted Richard to do his hat trick, and the Canadiens took a 3-1 lead with more than a minute of power play time entering the final period.

By this time, the Forum crowd went nuts every time Richard touched the puck, and he responded by scoring a power play goal, aided by his linemates and Irvin's crafty coaching. "Dick played Richard on all three lines," Carroll wrote. "Half the time Richard was out there, Davidson was sitting on the bench. Rocket made a monkey out of the younger Leafs who tried to take over the task of shadowing him."

Sure enough, at 8:54 'Maurice the Magnificent' delivered Montreal's fifth and final goal, cementing the 5-1 win. Whether this was Richard's best game will always be open for debate, but the question was addressed that same night by Hall of Fame *Hockey Night in Canada* broadcaster Foster Hewitt. When asked to pick the game's three stars, Hewitt answered, "First star: Maurice Richard. Second star: Maurice Richard. Third star: Maurice Richard!"

Others summed up the score this way: Richard 5, Toronto 1. But no matter how you score it, the Canadiens ousted Toronto in five and then Chicago in four to give The Rocket his first Stanley Cup.

Not too bad for a kid they once said was too brittle to be a big-leaguer.

BY STAN FISCHLER

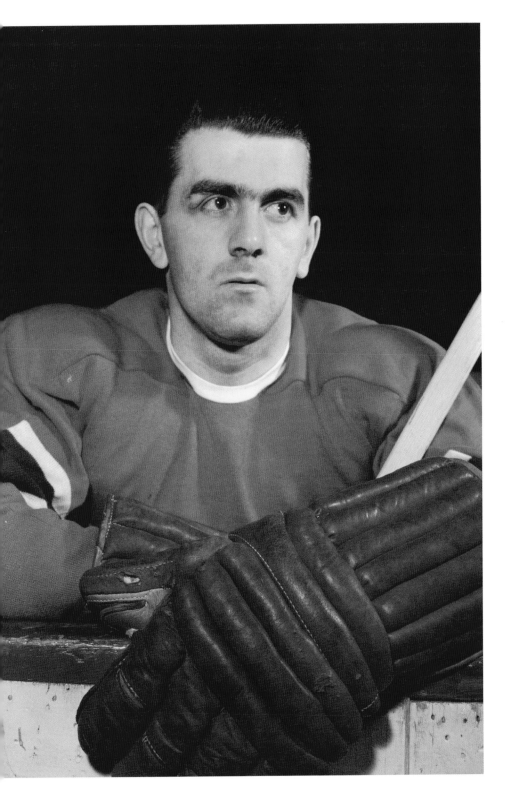

BEN SCRIVENS

JANUARY 29, 2014

EDMONTON 3 vs. SAN JOSE 0

•••

Take a stab at who you think might own the record for most saves in a regulation shutout. Roy? Try again. Hasek? Nope. The answer is as odd as the goaltender himself.

"You never know how it's going to go. You can have a terrible warmup and a terrible game, a great warmup and a terrible game, a great warmup and a great game. That night, I had a terrible warmup and a great game."

—Ben Scrivens

When Ben Scrivens awoke on Jan. 29, 2014, it was snowing lightly in Edmonton and the temperature was -13 degrees Fahrenheit. Even though he had been basking in the California sun just two weeks earlier, he was no stranger to chilly temperatures – he had grown up down the road in Spruce Grove.

He would go on to make history that evening, but at that moment, he said, it was just another workday. "It's silly to have premonitional thoughts," Scrivens said. "You're asking for trouble if you're trying to predict what's going to happen in the future. It was just a normal game day."

Scrivens is quick to point out that his normal is different from many goaltenders'. "I'm fairly loose," he said. "It probably doesn't help my case much, looking at it from an outsider's perspective. In general, coaches and management at this level don't understand the position and what it entails. They like what they know, and I'm definitely a contrarian in many aspects of my life. I don't check all the boxes."

Scrivens doesn't skate on the morning of a game, preferring to conserve his energy for the

real deal. He has lunch and a nap and tries to relax. After the pre-game meeting, there's a snack, some stretching, and then it's game time.

As he prepared to meet the San Jose Sharks that day, a team that was on its way to a second-place finish in the Pacific Division, he wasn't concerned by the fact that things didn't feel quite right going into the game. "I had a terrible warm-up," Scrivens recalled. "I didn't stop a thing. But I've learned that a warmup doesn't reflect what the game becomes. I'm out there to get a sweat going."

Scrivens started the season in Los Angeles as the backup to Jonathan Quick, making a strong early impression by posting a 6-1-3 record, before Quick suffered a groin injury in November. Scrivens had a 1.97 goals-against average for the Kings with a .931 save percentage through 19 games, and that should have given him a measure of security.

But rookie Martin Jones was even better in Quick's absence. He won his first eight NHL games, posting a 1.00 GAA, a .966 SP and three shutouts in the process. When Quick returned, Scrivens became redundant. On Jan. 15, he was traded to Edmonton for a third-round draft pick. The Oilers were desperate for help between the pipes.

When Scrivens took the ice on Jan. 29, it was just his fourth start for the Oilers, and he stepped onto the ice looking like a beer league player with an incomplete set of gear. He still had his Kings' helmet and also wore gloves and pads with L.A. colors.

When the puck was dropped to start the game, Scrivens left the awful warmup behind, and it wasn't long before he had made what would be the first save of a record 59 in a 3-0 shutout win. "It's a cliché, but I was just focusing on one shot at a time," said Scrivens. "There wasn't a time where I felt I was in a 'zone' or I was making history. There's a storytelling aspect for the fans and the media, but when you're out there, you never know how it's going to finish. There was an awkward save I made early in the first. I came across, and the shooter had it on his backhand. He flipped it up, and I got my blocker on it as I was falling backward. To be able to track that shot and battle through, that's kind of a confidence thing. From there, you settle in and wait for the next shot."

And there were a lot of "next shots." In addition to the 59 on goal – an NHL record for the most saves in a regulation shutout – the Oilers blocked 22 shots and 19 others were off target, for a total of 100 attempts. "San Jose had a good team, and there was never any time to relax," said Scrivens, who had set a personal best of 42 saves after two periods alone. He stopped Patrick Marleau on a breakaway late in the second period and on four other shots, and he frustrated Brent Burns, who led the Sharks with eight shots on goal.

Scrivens wasn't aware that he had even set a record until he was mobbed by the media after the game. "I did my interviews after the game and somebody from the media filled me in," Scrivens said. "I didn't look at the total when I was on the ice. I knew it was up there, but the only thing I cared about was that I had a shutout, and we won."

BY PAT HICKEY

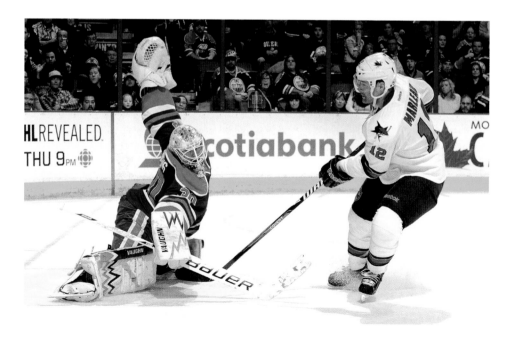

KIMBI DANIELS

 ## SWIFT CURRENT 7 VS. MEDICINE HAT 4

•••

Any player would be proud of a hat trick, which is what Daniels had when he left the game for the dressing room. It's a good thing he took the advice of a trainer, though, because upon his return Daniels played his way into WHL history.

"I guess from a statistical standpoint it was my greatest game. I probably felt I may have played better games with less numbers, but it was just one of those days when everything seemed to fall into place."
—Kimbi Daniels

Kimbi Daniels thought his night was over. While killing a penalty in the second period for the Swift Current Broncos, the then 17-year-old blocked a point shot with his right foot. And it hurt, badly. He left the game immediately and went to the dressing room. Daniels was convinced his foot was broken.

But the trainer told him to walk it off, keep the skate on and see how it felt. After roughly five more minutes of game time had passed, Daniels returned to give one of the WHL's best single-game goal-scoring performances.

In the history of the league, five players have scored seven goals in a game, but the first four to complete the task (Brian Propp, Ray Ferraro, Mark Mackay and Dennis Holland) did it in laughers and blowouts. Their teams won big, and the seven-goal scorers were the highlight of a constellation of offensive stars.

Daniels was the only Swift Current Bronco to find the back of the net in a 7-4 win against the Medicine Hat Tigers on Oct. 2, 1990. And he almost had an eighth goal. Medicine Hat was attempting to pull goalie Chris Osgood for an extra

attacker when Daniels intercepted a pass. He carried it into the offensive zone uncontested, but Osgood, who had reversed course, skated as fast as he could and dove at Daniels' feet. "He tripped me," Daniels said. "Otherwise, I would have had eight and the record."

It was the only thing that didn't go Daniels' way on a day that started as a "typical Tuesday night in October" and ended with seven goals while his dad, Louis, was in attendance.

Before he blocked the shot and missed some of the action, he already had three goals. When he returned he scored four more, including three on the power play.

Although the scoresheet said otherwise, the Swift Current offense wasn't built around Daniels that night. Teammates weren't going out of their way to set him up (that would have been irresponsible in what was then a close game), and Daniels wasn't a high-volume shooter. "I was always a pass-first guy, even in that game," Daniels said. "I remember the goals came from being in the right areas – I think one was a breakaway – but the rest were just from going to the net and being in the right spot at the right time."

Speaking of being at the right place and right time, check out the 1990-91 Seventh Inning Sketch WHL hockey card set. A photographer made the trip to Medicine Hat to take headshots of both teams after the game for the trading card company. Daniels posed for the generic, run-of-the-mill headshot like his teammates and then took another – this one while holding all seven pucks from his momentous night. "Everyone else got one card that season," Daniels said. "I got two."

As expected, Daniels' foot swelled up like a balloon once he removed his skate. It ended up being a deep bone bruise that forced him to miss a couple days of practice. Rather than have the seven-goal scorer stop back at the rink and hobble his way home, the bus went straight from Medicine Hat to Daniels' residence. It was on a cul-de-sac and it was almost 1 a.m. when the bus rolled in. "I'm sure it woke up some of the neighbors," Daniels said. "But it sure saved me the hassle of having to pack my bag and drive home."

BY SEAN SHAPIRO

JIM MONTGOMERY

--- APRIL 3, 1993 ---

MAINE 5 VS. LAKE SUPERIOR STATE 4

•••

**In the final period of his final game as a Black Bear, Montgomery made
sure Maine went out on a high note, as the team's pep band played host Wisconsin's
signature tune to get Badger fans on their side against the Lakers.**

*"The dressing room was calm. Justin Tomberlin stood up and said, 'You know what?
Jimmy's line hasn't scored yet, and that hasn't happened all year.' "*
—Jim Montgomery

The University of Maine was supposed to win the Frozen Four in 1992, but a first-round upset at the hands of Michigan State denied the Black Bears the championship they so fervently desired. So even with future NHLer Scott Pellerin off the roster heading into the next campaign, the Black Bears were no less resolute in what they wanted to accomplish. "We had seven seniors who had been through so much," said high-flying center Jim Montgomery. "Before the year started, we said that we weren't going to leave any stone unturned. We weren't going to leave anything to chance."

A legendary recruiting class that summer helped the proclamation, with the highly touted Ferraro twins, Chris and Peter, coming in. Also making his debut in Orono: a new linemate for Montgomery, a kid from British Columbia named Paul Kariya.

The incredibly skilled left winger would go on to win the Hobey Baker Award in his first season, and in the process he and Montgomery made magic. When the Black Bears needed those guys the most, they came through. Trailing Lake Superior State 4-2 in the national title game, Montgomery netted a natural hat trick, with the

aid of Kariya, and Maine had its first men's hockey championship.

Even though they were a team that had lost just one game all season, the Black Bears still had drama in the Frozen Four. A disputed no-goal call against Michigan in the semifinal meant that Maine had to go to overtime to take out the Wolverines. But legendary coach Shawn Walsh had some tricks up his sleeve to get the crowd on his side.

That year, the Frozen Four was hosted by the University of Wisconsin, at the Bradley Center in Milwaukee. The Badgers had been knocked out in overtime by that same Michigan squad in the West regional, so Walsh had Maine's pep band learn the school fight song, "On Wisconsin." Needless to say, the locals took a shine to the Black Bears for those final two games.

But the Lakers were a formidable opponent, nonetheless. In fact, they were the defending national champions thanks to future NHLer Brian Rolston, stellar coaching from Jeff Jackson and a burly lineup. "They were a heavy team," Montgomery said. "They were a cycle team, and they played the left-wing lock on the forecheck."

So despite Maine jumping out to a 2-0 lead in the first period, Lake Superior pushed its way back into the driver's seat with four straight goals as the teams headed into the final intermission. You'd think the Black Bears would have been worried at that point, but Montgomery paints a different scene. It was a calm, confident group that came together before the third period began. And as it turned out, the offensive stars led the way.

Montgomery's line with Kariya and Cal Ingraham had ventilated the opposition all year long, with the trio combining for an astounding 280 points over the course of the 45-game season. They hadn't scored yet in the game, but that was all about to change.

Montgomery's first goal came early on a pinpoint pass from Kariya. "I could have put the puck in the net with a pool cue," he said. The second came off a shot that deflected off a Lake Superior defenseman's stick, while Montgomery's hat trick goal came with 11 minutes remaining. Starting with the puck behind his own goalie, Montgomery skated up the ice before dishing it to Kariya, who returned the favor for a pass that was almost a carbon copy of the one that had given Montgomery his first goal.

As incredible as the chemistry was between the two silky forwards, Montgomery points out another wrinkle in Maine's strategy that helped the Black Bears out in the third period.

While starter Mike Dunham made some excellent saves against Lake Superior, he was replaced after 40 minutes by Garth Snow (the two future NHLers shared duty all season). One of the upshots of having Snow in the crease for the final stanza was that he was one of the best puckhandling goalies in the game. That greatly helped Maine break Lake Superior's trap and proved especially important down the stretch when the Black Bears were protecting that perilous one-goal lead. Snow also ended up making some insane saves near the end and survived a close call

on a Sean Tallaire shot that rang off the crossbar when the goalie was prone.

Montgomery admitted that the Black Bears did start to play nervously as the Lakers continued to push for that tying goal. And with about two minutes left, a crucial decision had to be made. His line was tired, but Lake Superior was sending out their top unit, led by Rolston. Montgomery pleaded with coach Walsh to call a timeout so he and his linemates could stay out. Walsh didn't want to do it, but Montgomery was adamant, and the coach relented. "If we were going to lose," Montgomery said, "we were going to do it with our best players on the ice."

Sure enough, the dam held. Even with Lake Superior goalie Blaine Lacher pulled for an extra attacker, the Lakers couldn't pierce Snow in net. The final seconds ticked down with most of the play confined to the neutral zone, and the celebration was on – Maine had its title. "It was the first time the state had accomplished anything like that," Montgomery said. "It was finally accomplishing what we all came to Maine to do."

So those seven seniors found their glory. Kariya left during his sophomore season to play for the Canadian national team and never returned. In the immediate aftermath, however, there was some partying to do. The nearby convention center featured 1,000 Maine fans waiting for their hockey heroes, and the place went nuts when the team arrived. It was a long night and a fun one. "It was a blur," Montgomery said. "But we were together the whole time."

In retrospect, it's hard to imagine a team like Maine in modern hockey – Jack Eichel was a dominant force in 2014-15 for Boston University, and even he couldn't come close to the 100 points that Kariya put up as a freshman. And having two No. 1 goalies, both of whom would go on to the NHL? That's pretty outstanding, too. "It was a culmination," Montgomery said. "We had the best coaching staff, we had the best goalie tandem

> "IF WE WERE GOING TO LOSE, WE WERE GOING TO DO IT WITH OUR BEST PLAYERS ON THE ICE."

in the NCAA, and we had the best college player ever."

But if it wasn't for Montgomery finishing those Kariya passes in that tour-de-force third-period performance, the Black Bears wouldn't have that 1993 banner at all.

BY RYAN KENNEDY

JOE MALONE

JANUARY 31, 1920

QUEBEC 10 VS. TORONTO 6

TORONTO
ST PATS

●●●

On a cold winter's night, as fans sat down to watch the two worst teams in the league duke it out, nobody could have predicted that they were going to witness one of the longest-standing records in NHL history.

"I didn't have the hardest shot in the world.
But I knew where it was going most of the time."
—Joe Malone

Joe Malone was the greatest goal scorer of his day – of that there is no doubt. Malone had the type of numbers that jump off the page, no matter the era. The Quebec-born Montreal native scored at a clip of 1.45 goals per game in the National Hockey Association, followed by 1.13 per game in seven NHL seasons. Just to put that into perspective, the best goal scorer in recent years, Alex Ovechkin, has scored at a pace of 0.63 goals per game over the course of his career. Wayne Gretzky scored at a pace of 0.6 goals per game (though the guy also had a few assists). So, yeah, Malone knew how to put the puck in the net.

The game has certainly changed since Malone played hockey, from 1911 to 1924. He may not have played with pucks made of frozen cow dung, but almost everything else about the game was different. The equipment was primitive: flat wooden sticks kept the puck low, goalies were asked to make saves wearing minimal protection and arenas featured poor lighting and even questionable ice. Forward-passing was only allowed in the neutral zone, slowing the game down, and the superstars would often play the full 60 minutes. "We had a lot of ice time," Malone said in an interview with *The Hockey News* in 1961. "But I'll tell you, we didn't go up and down the rink like they do today. We'd hustle when opportunities presented, and then we'd loaf. At least I did. It was the only way you could go the 60 minutes, and a lot of players had to do that."

'Phantom Joe' Malone was certainly one of those superstars. His name filled the record books at the time, though many of those have since been shattered – most notably his 44 goals in a season and his 14 consecutive games with a goal. (Malone's streak came in his first taste of the NHL, which is still the best mark at the start of a career.) But there are some records that are never meant to be broken.

On Jan. 31, 1920, Malone took the ice for the Quebec Bulldogs against the Toronto St. Patricks. The game received very little attention, since these two cellar dwellers were facing off while Montreal battled for a playoff spot in Ottawa. It was also the coldest night of the Quebec winter, a night on which only 1,200 people came out to the game. But it was money well spent for those fans, who witnessed one of the greatest individual goal-scoring performances in NHL history.

Malone only scored one goal in the first period, but managed a hat trick in the second period. With the Bulldogs up 7-6 in the third and killing a major penalty, Malone potted two goals shorthanded to keep the game out of reach. Phantom Joe scored his record-setting seventh goal late in the game, leaving his mark on a 10-6 Bulldogs win.

Seven goals in one game – imagine the pandemonium that would ensue if that happened today. In 1920, however, it received very little attention. This was a game of little consequence in the standings, and performances like these weren't uncommon, especially for Malone. Just six weeks later, Malone would score six against Ottawa in Quebec's last game of the season, and by the time his NHL career started he had racked up some impressive performances in the NHA – a seven- and an eight-goal game, and even a nine-goal Stanley Cup-winning game in 1913.

It is no wonder, then, that Malone is the earliest player featured in *The Hockey News'* Top 100 Greatest NHL Players of All Time, coming in at No. 39. His seven-goal feat has stood the test of time: 52,765 regular season games have been played since, not counting the 2016-17 season. Only three players have scored six goals in a game since: Syd Howe in 1944, Red Berenson in 1968 and Darryl Sittler in his famous 10-point performance in 1976. No player has had more games with five or more goals than Malone's five. Wayne Gretzky and Mario Lemieux came the closest with four apiece.

Phantom Joe's best skills were his smooth stickhandling and his skating. It was said that Malone was born before his time. Had he played alongside Maurice Richard and company in the 1940s and 1950s, there's no telling how many goals he might have scored. Malone retired in 1924 after a brief stint with the Canadiens, saying he knew it was time. "I took a look at a new kid in our training camp at Grimsby, Ont., and knew right then I was ready for the easy chair. He was Howie Morenz. In practice he moved past me so fast I thought I was standing still. I knew it was time to quit."

It's worth noting that Malone led the league in scoring during the 1919-20 season, putting up 39 goals despite playing on a horrendous Quebec team that finished 4-20. How bad were the Bulldogs? Their goaltender Frank Brophy set the NHL record for worst goals-against average, putting up a shocking 7.11 GAA in 21 games. The fact that Quebec won any games is a testament to Malone's goal scoring abilities, though in true hockey player fashion he was typically modest of his record-setting seven-goal game: "I guess I was just lucky."

"WE'D HUSTLE WHEN OPPORTUNITIES PRESENTED, AND THEN WE'D LOAF. AT LEAST I DID."

BY JACOB COHEN

QUEBEC
Stanley Cup Champions — 1912

Top Row—left to right: L. LAGUEUX (Committee) C. FREMONT (Committee) T. B. O'NIEL (Committee)
A. DEROME (Committee) F. HILL (Committee)

Second Row: C. LOCKWELL (Committee) C. NOLAN (Coach) D. BELAND (Trainer) G. LEONARD G. CAREY
J. SAVARD J. E. MATTE (Treasurer)

Third Row: B. J. KAINE (Secretary) Hon. P. A. CHOQUETTE (President) W. ROONEY G. PRODGER J. MALONE (Captain)
J. HALL P. MORAN M. J. QUINN (Vice-President) (Manager)

Bottom Row: J. MARKS J. McDONALD

Inset: E. OATMAN

KIM MARTIN

FEBRUARY 17, 2006

SWEDEN 3 VS. UNITED STATES 2

•••

A seasoned veteran led the way offensively against the heavily favored United States, but it was an ice-cold teenager who barred the barn door in net to complete Sweden's "mirakel" on ice.

"That's when we all thought, 'This is possible.' But I was so focused I didn't even have time to think. I was completely in the zone. It's not often we scored twice."
—Kim Martin

K im Martin knew what was at stake. Veteran Maria Rooth had single-handedly staged a comeback for Sweden, scoring twice in under four minutes in the second period to tie Sweden's semifinal game against the United States at the 2006 Olympics. A win would send the Swedes to the gold medal game and etch their name in hockey history.

Martin had already stopped 25 of 27 shots through two periods, while her teammates had managed just nine, and she knew the Americans would keep coming. So between the second and third periods, Martin practised her modus operandi. Calm was Martin's armor, impenetrable neither by the crowd of 5,654 fans at Torino's Palasport Olimpico nor by the nerves involved in the chance to upset one of the two powerhouses in women's hockey. "It was fairly calm during the intermission," Martin said. "Great leaders brought our team together."

It was a tall order for a teenager to fill, though Martin, 11 days shy of her 20th birthday, was no stranger to backstopping winners. After all, she had helped Sweden to bronze against their archrival Finland four years prior at the 2002 Olympics in Salt Lake City, U.S. So Martin knew what was at stake, but she remained grounded thanks to her routine. "I've never done anything too crazy before games: eat, warmup, chat, play – nothing crazy at all, very normal, especially for a goalie," Martin said. "I like doing the same stuff, but if I miss something, I stay pretty levelheaded and don't let it get to me."

Sweden's shot at advancing to the final really sank in for Martin after her teammates killed off a tripping penalty to Danijela Rundqvist in overtime. By the time the buzzer sounded to end overtime and signal a shootout, Martin had stopped another 12 shots, facing 39 in total for the game. She then denied all three American sharpshooters in the shootout – Natalie Derwitz, Angela Ruggiero and Krissy Wendell. Rooth then continued her heroics, scoring her third of the night in the shootout to complete the upset over the U.S. The headline in *Sports Illustrated* was the Swedish word "Mirakel."

Although Sweden ultimately fell to Canada in the gold medal game, Martin looks back on her team's unlikely run with a tranquil pride: "That silver was as good as gold for us."

BY MONIKA MORAVAN

PATRIK LAINE & JESSE PULJUJARVI

FINLAND 4 VS. RUSSIA 3

•••

What are Finnish men made of? Thick skin to keep out the cold and steely determination in the face of adversity. Two teenagers put that fully on display at the 2016 World Junior Championship in their greatest game as teammates.

"I kept asking, 'Is this real? Are we truly champions?'"
—Patrik Laine

"I couldn't believe it was true."
—Jesse Puljujarvi

The earliest days of 2016 were freezing in Finland. The Nordic country and its capital, Helsinki, had been buried in snow and frost since Christmas. There were only short periods of daylight, but there was one place that was boiling hot.

Hartwall Arena, the main rink for the 2016 World Junior Championship, had been blessed with the magical performances of a pair of young men: Patrik Laine and Jesse Puljujarvi. The pair – Finland's deadliest weapons in the tournament – had dominated the scoresheet, prompting even the Finns in the audience to wonder aloud about the possibility of a gold medal.

Not only were they the hottest athletes at the tournament, they had become some of the hottest celebrities in the country, and everyone came to know them by their nicknames: 'Pate' and 'Pulju'. The two had mesmerized the hockey world over the holidays, and in Finland they were the golden kids who could do no wrong. "At first there was practically nothing," Laine said. "But as the tournament progressed,

the media attention grew bigger and bigger all the time."

Finland had beaten Canada and Sweden in the medal round and was facing Russia in the final. They had lost to the Russians 6-4 in the round-robin, however, casting a foreboding shadow over the upcoming gold medal game. But those three tough matches had prepared the Young Lions for this ultimate challenge.

Laine and Puljujarvi were not only good friends and linemates, they were also roommates during the tournament. They started game day just like any other by going to breakfast. But as the day wore on, they began to reflect on the weight of the upcoming challenge. "The day felt so long," Laine said. "There was so much time to spend. We had to think of all kinds of things. One more win and we are world champions. The feeling was good, but somehow strange at the same time."

Despite the frigid weather outside, there was nothing cold about the game itself. The arena was full, and the entire country hoped and prayed for gold. The home crowd got some help from Canadian fans who were supporting the host nation after losing to Finland in the quarterfinal. "In principle, it was just a game among others," Puljujarvi said. "But occasionally, I had time to think, 'Wow, the final game is ahead.' "

Russia jumped out to an early lead, forcing Finland to chase the game all the way into the third period. Then Laine, the team's leading scorer in the tournament, evened the score thanks in part to an assist from Puljujarvi. "The feeling was even better than when I had scored," Laine said.

Russia took hold of the lead again on the next shift, but the wunderkinds struck back. Laine checked a Russian defenseman off the puck, and Puljujarvi picked it up and found center Sebastian Aho in front of the net. "It felt as good as if I had scored the goal myself," Puljujarvi said.

> **"FOR THE FIRST TIME THAT DAY, I THOUGHT FOR A MOMENT THAT THERE WAS A CHANCE WE COULD ACTUALLY LOSE THE GAME."**

With 10 minutes to go, the score was tied 2-2. Then, at 57:51, Mikko Rantanen sent Finland into a frenzy, deflecting a Vili Saarijarvi shot into the Russian net. "I thought, 'Now we could actually win, now we are close,' " Puljujarvi said. "However, at the same time, we had to keep in mind that we weren't there yet."

With two minutes to go and gold within reach, the clock tormented the Finns as the seconds seemed slow. Then, with Puljujarvi and Laine sitting next to each other on the bench, watching the team's checking line battle against the goal-hungry Russians, the unthinkable happened.

Six seconds before they would have been saved by the bell, Russia scored the tying goal. "I've never been so nervous – I was anxious as hell," Puljujarvi said. "Then, for the first time that day, I thought for a moment that there was a chance we could actually lose the game."

"I thought, 'Is it over?' " Laine said. "Luckily, the break came quickly and we got the troops gathered again."

The Finnish dressing room was tense even as players tried to pump each other up.

The names of those who were most nervous during intermission remain unknown, but everyone knows the name of the hero who scored the golden goal.

Kasperi Kapanen's overtime winner lifted the snow-covered roof off of the arena. The rest of the Finnish population jumped for joy in front of their televisions, practically shaking the ice from the branches in nearby trees. "When Kasperi was behind the goal with the puck, I thought for a second 'Now he can score,' " Puljujarvi said. "When I saw the puck go in, at first I couldn't believe it. We just jumped up from the bench and started to celebrate. We got up so fast that I still can't believe it. When we chased Kasperi, I just remember shouting as loud as I possibly could."

Laine's first seconds as a world champion were just as loud, but also slightly painful. "Our bench got so crowded all of a sudden that my foot got stuck on the side of the boards," Laine said. "So when I jumped over, I landed on the ice on my face."

When Finland wins gold in hockey, the following happens: The streets are flooded with people celebrating and dancing, splashing in the fountains – yes, even in January – and Helsinki's market square comes alive. The Young Lions got their party, too. After a sleepless night, the square of Helsinki Olympic Stadium was transformed into festival grounds. It was -13 degrees Fahrenheit, but nobody cared. Thousands of people came out, and about one million Finns watched it from their homes. The audience was young, as were the players, and the players were treated like rock stars.

Laine summed up the moment perfectly. "I hope that I can experience that kind of thing again someday," he said. "Perhaps the Stanley Cup could be as great a thing to achieve as this was."

BY PANU MARKKANEN

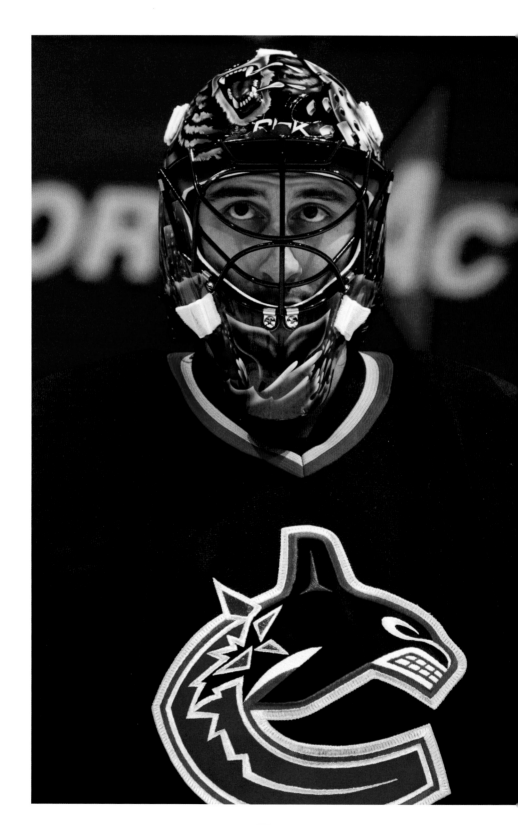

ROBERTO LUONGO

APRIL 11, 2007

VANCOUVER 5 VS. DALLAS 4

•••

**Almost 10 years after being drafted, Luongo finally got a taste
of post-season hockey, but nothing could have prepared him for the task
he would face in the first playoff game of his career.**

*"I remember a player came with a wraparound, and I was so tired that I fell on the ice and
was just holding my skate against the post. The guy jammed at it four times. I have no idea
how it didn't go in. I didn't have the energy to hold the post there. Then we scored."*
—Roberto Luongo

Before his first NHL playoff game in 2007, Roberto Luongo flew some friends into Vancouver to share the Stanley Cup post-season experience with him. No one could have predicted they would be at the arena as long as they were. "They were dying," Luongo said.

Luongo's first foray into the NHL's big dance was one of the longest playoff games in history, a marathon that lasted into the following day before Henrik Sedin finally lifted the Canucks to a 5-4 win over Dallas. The opening-round game lasted over five hours, with Luongo making 72 saves in the span of four overtimes – one shy of the NHL record set by Kelly Hrudey almost 20 years prior.

No other goalie in their first playoff game had fought off so much rubber. After it was all over, Luongo collapsed on a training table deep inside Vancouver's GM Place. He said he could have slept for days – yet that wasn't an option. The second game of the series was less than 42 hours away. "It was so exhausting," Luongo says now, almost 10 years later. "I had never been through anything like that before. And I haven't been through anything like that since. I was completely drained."

When Luongo was traded from the Islanders to Florida at the 2000 NHL Draft, the Panthers had just been swept by the Devils, later to be Cup champions, in the first round.

Luongo came to Florida and was hailed as the team's newest hero, a budding superstar who was going to lead the Panthers into the post-season for years and years to come. Things sometimes don't work out as planned, though. After five seasons with the Panthers, Luongo never made it past Game 82, and the Panthers never came close to making the playoffs during what would be his first tenure there.

In 2006, there was a rift between Luongo and management – especially general manager Mike Keenan. Keenan had his mind set on getting rid of Luongo, and with the draft being held in Vancouver, Keenan pulled off a blockbuster of a deal. The night before the draft was to start, Luongo was traded – and he was going to the Canucks.

Local fans celebrated the acquisition of Luongo by taking to the streets. Some created makeshift jerseys to wear to the draft at GM Place. On draft day, Keenan reveled in the adulation of the Vancouver faithful, raising his arms to the sky as he walked along the draft floor to a rousing standing ovation.

The trade wasn't as popular back in Florida. A few months after Keenan traded Luongo away, he was fired.

For Luongo, the trade meant a fresh start in a different situation. Now in the spotlight before a hockey-hungry audience, he tried to do things as he did before. His preparation remained the same, and he kept his attention on the finer points of his game.

The Canucks qualified fourth in the Western Conference in 2007 as Luongo excelled in his western transition. During the season, Luongo won 47 games and had what was then a career-best 2.29 goals-against average. The playoffs, Luongo would soon find out, are a different animal. "I was nervous, no doubt about it," Luongo said. "I had been waiting a long time for that one moment. I had been in the league a while and had been waiting a long time to be a part of something like that. There were a lot of emotions running through me at the time."

> ## "I HAD NEVER BEEN THROUGH ANYTHING LIKE THAT BEFORE. AND I HAVEN'T BEEN THROUGH ANYTHING LIKE THAT SINCE. I WAS COMPLETELY DRAINED."

Luongo's first playoff game started well enough: Daniel Sedin opened the scoring four minutes in. Dallas' Brenden Morrow quickly answered. With less than 12 minutes left, Vancouver held a 4-2 lead, which would have been enough during the regular season. Luongo would have slammed the door, and everyone would have gone out to celebrate. But the Stars kept coming and scored twice in a span of just over five minutes in the third. "I don't even remember that," Luongo said.

Overtime in the Stanley Cup playoffs is as exciting a moment as there is in sports. Score and you win, perhaps moving on to bigger and better things. Give up that goal, and not only is a game lost but so, too, could be a season. "The play definitely tightened up," Luongo said. "That was fun hockey."

Luongo and Dallas' Marty Turco matched save for save as the overtime periods came and went. During intermissions, Luongo tried to stay fresh by eating oranges, the juice giving him a needed boost of energy. His teammates, many of whom had not eaten since lunch, broke into the post-game spread, which was now cold, since it had been brought in during the third period. Players in various stages of undress trying to recover for the next overtime period chowed down on room-temperature pizza. Luongo stuck with the citrus and an energy bar – "Or two," Luongo recalled. "After the second overtime, we were just laughing. 'When is this going to end?' "

The fourth overtime period, like the three before it, was wracked with tension. Luongo and Turco waited each other out. One was going to blink first, but who?

With less than two minutes remaining in the fourth overtime and on Vancouver's 34th shot since regulation ended, Henrik Sedin mercifully ended it. After two hours, 18 minutes and six seconds of game time, Luongo and the Canucks had won the opening game of their series. Any questions about whether Luongo was ready for such a stage vanished. "I got all the experience I needed in one game," he quipped afterward.

Back home in Quebec, it was after 3 a.m. and many of Luongo's friends and family members who hadn't been able to travel to British Columbia were going wild. Luongo, however, was in no mood to party. "It was just a crazy game," he said. "I had to get ready for Game 2 and remember playing in that one and still being exhausted. It was so long, so stressful. It took all my energy. Just crazy. It was great."

BY GEORGE RICHARDS

173

PHOTO CREDITS

06 Bob Shaver/Hockey Hall of Fame
08 Graig Abel/NHLI via Getty Images
13 Bennett Studios/Getty Images
14 Ovechkin_Crosby4: Bruce Bennett/Getty Images
17 Len Redkoles/Getty Images
18 Richard Wolowicz/Getty Images
20 Andre Ringuette/HHOF-IIHF Images
21 Richard Wolowicz/Getty Images
22 HHOF-IIHF Images
26 John Giamundo/Getty Images
29 Robert Laberge/ALLSPORT
30 Cameron Spencer/Getty Images
33 Bruce Bennett/Getty Images
34 Graphic Artists/Hockey Hall of Fame
37 Paul Bereswill/Hockey Hall of Fame
38 Christopher Pasatieri/Getty Images
41 Christopher Pasatieri/Getty Images
42 Quebec Remparts
44 Quebec Remparts
45 Steve Babineau/NHLI via Getty Images
46 Bruce Bennett Studios/Getty Images
48 Philadelphia Flyers
49 Philadelphia Flyers
50 B Bennett/Getty Images
52 Anthony Neste/Sports Illustrated/Getty Images
53 B Bennett/Getty Images
54 Glenn Cratty/Allsport
57 Glenn Cratty/Allsport
58 Ron Bull/Toronto Star via Getty Images
61 Ron Bull/Toronto Star via Getty Images
63 Steve Russell/Toronto Star via Getty Images
64 O-Pee-Chee/HHOF collection
67 THN Archives
68 Jeff Goode/Toronto Star via Getty Images
71 Frank Lennon/Toronto Star via Getty Images
72 John Tlumacki/The Boston Globe via
   Getty Images
75 John Tlumacki/The Boston Globe via
   Getty Images
76 Steve Babineau/NHLI via Getty Images
78 Bruce Bennett Studios/Getty Images
79 Steve Babineau/NHLI via Getty Images
80 B Bennett/Getty Images
83 B Bennett/Getty Images
84-85 Paul Bereswill/Hockey Hall of Fame
86 Ben Dodds/BLD Graphics
88 Ben Dodds/BLD Graphics
89 Ben Dodds/BLD Graphics
90 B Bennett/Getty Images
92 B Bennett/Getty Images
93 David E. Klutho /Sports Illustrated/
   Getty Images

94 Doug Pensinger/Allsport
95 Glenn Cratty/Allsport
96 Ian Tomlinson/Allsport
98 Providence College Athletics
101 Providence College Athletics
102 Robert Laberge/Getty Images
105 David E. Klutho /Sports Illustrated/
   Getty Images
106 HHOF Images
109 Bruce Bennett Studios/Getty Images
110 Dave Sandford/NHLI via Getty Images
113 Gregory Shamus/NHLI via Getty Images
114 Dave Reginek/NHLI via Getty Images
115 Doug Pensinger/Allsport
118 Mark Sandten/Bongarts/Getty Images
119 OLIVIER MORIN/AFP/Getty Images
120 Nat Turofsky/HHOF Images
122 B Bennett/Getty Images
123 HHOF Images
124 Andy Devlin/NHLI via Getty Images
125 Andy Devlin/NHLI via Getty Images
126 Andy Devlin/NHLI via Getty Images
128 Hockey Canada Images
131 Hockey Canada Images
132 Steve Babineau/NHLI via Getty Images
134 Aaron Ontiveroz/ The Denver Post
137 Doug Pensinger/Getty Images
138 Graig Abel Collection/Getty Images
141 Graig Abel Collection/Getty Images
142 HHOF Images
144 Pictorial Parade/Getty Images
147 Frank Prazak/HHOF Images
148 Derek Leung/Getty Images
150 Andy Devlin/NHLI via Getty Images
151 Andy Devlin/NHLI via Getty Images
152 HHOF Images
154 HHOF Images
155 WHL
156 University of Maine Athletics
159 University of Maine Athletics
160 James Rice/Hockey Hall of Fame
163 B Bennett/Getty Images
164 Corey Sipkin/NY Daily News Archive via
   Getty Images
166 Andre Ringuette/HHOF-IIHF Images
169 Andre Ringuette/HHOF-IIHF Images
170 Jeff Vinnick/Getty Images
173 Jeff Vinnick/Getty Images
174 Damian Strohmeyer /Sports Illustrated/
   Getty Images

ACKNOWLEDGMENTS

• • •

Thanks abound for what was truly a team effort:

To *The Hockey News*' management team – Sandra Martin, publisher, Jason Kay, editor in chief, and Edward Fraser, managing editor – for all of their work behind the scenes.

Leanne Gilbert, THN's art director, for her vision and guidance.

Colin Elliott, Carlie McGhee, Sylvana Sciortino, Amanda Usher and Angela Valentini, THN's marketing/communications team, for getting the word out across the hockey world.

THN staffers, Ken Campbell, Jared Clinton, Brian Costello, Ian Denomme, Ryan Kennedy and Matt Larkin, for weaving some wicked yarns.

Freelance writers Shelly Anderson, Sal Barry, Uffe Bodin, Mike Brophy, Jason Buckland, Rich Chere, Bob Duff, Josh Elliott, Stan Fischler, Wayne Fish, Denis Gibbons, Stu Hackel, Pat Hickey, Dhiren Mahiban, Panu Markkanen, John Matisz, Sarah McLellan, Brian McNally, Monika Moravan, Daniel Nugent-Bowman, Paul Patskou, David Pollak, Adam Proteau, George Richards, Jeremy Rutherford, Sean Shapiro, Robin Short, Randy Sportak, Eric Stephens, Rob Tychkowski, Scott Wheeler, Michael Willhoft and Eric Zweig, for their expertise and coverage.

Fearless fact-checkers Casey Ippolito and Malcolm Campbell, for exorcizing all of the devils hiding in the dirty details.

Rachel Villari, for her careful copy editing, and Luke Sawczak, for his precise proofreading.

And THN's cast of intrepid interns, Chris Ciligot, Jacob Cohen, Matthew Cranker, Michael Fletcher, Jimmy Huynh, Emma Mason, Julia Robinson and Matthew Stamper, for all of their hard work from beginning to end.

Printed by Imprimerie Transcontinental, Beauceville, Canada